This book captures the fan Christian fellowship Fred a AFA. It was exciting for u tradition there, and it has be .... to watch Fred continue to rebuild programs everywhere he coaches. -- Chan Gailey Buffalo Bills head coach

Fred is one of a kind. Fred is a caring father and father figure, an aggressive and tough coach, and a leader with talented and supportive staffs. I immensely enjoyed the many colorful people Fred encountered in his lifetime. This book is a fun and exciting journey. It is a must read for anyone… football coaches, saints, and sinners. All will enjoy this book! -- Ken Hatfield, former head football coach Arkansas, Clemson, Rice, USAFA

Fred Goldsmith coached the game of football at a high level for more than 40 years. More important than his consistent success on the field, Fred left every program that he worked at better than he found it. Despite spending the majority of his head coaching career working at college programs (Rice University, Duke University, and Lenoir Rhyne) that were not traditional powers and that put a huge emphasis on academics, Fred achieved success while running his programs with integrity and doing things the right way. -- Rick Barnes, head basketball coach, University of Texas

Johnny, Thanks for your years of friendship, and all that you do for Jesus through FCA. God Bless Fred G

Fred was a great recruiter. He had a lot to do with me coming to the Academy. He called every night and made me think I was going to hell if I didn't come to the AFA. He made it sound like the next best place to heaven on earth. – Fisher DeBerry former head coach, USAFA

This book is an honest and transparent testimony of Coach Fred Goldsmith's life and coaching career. Fred received the Fellowship of Christian Athletes/Grant Teaff Lifetime Achievement Award in 2012. When you read his life story, you will clearly see why he received this honor. I encourage you to read and share this book, receive Christ as Fred did, and live each day making a difference.
 -- Dal Shealy, former FCA president

I learned long ago to measure coaches the same way I measure the beauty of my family – inside out. Coach Goldsmith has a heart and soul and mind unlike most. I hired him once, and I would hire him again. He did not put up all the numbers that every alumnus wanted but he touched the lives of hundreds of kids in a positive way. I've known a lot of good men. I've only had the privilege of knowing a few great men, but Goldsmith is in the latter group.
--Tom Butters, former AD Duke University

In five all too short seasons, Goldsmith rose to the rank of legend at Franklin High School. He molded young men into responsible students and football stars into championship contenders. His story will be told by townspeople for generations to come. It is a story of how one man made a huge difference in the life of his town, its residents, and his players.
--Barbara McRae *The Franklin Press*

This book is dedicated to Pam, Kim, Robin and all the coaches, players and staff who have become my extended family over the last 45 years.

COMEBACK COACH

FRED GOLDSMITH
Kimberly McDaniel

Table of Contents

	Foreword	6
1	The First Quarter	9
2	High School	14
3	College	18
4	High School Coaching Jobs	20
5	I'm So Glad I'm From FAMU	32
6	Off We Go Into the Wild Blue Yonder	38
7	Woo Pig Sooie	56
8	Why Not Rice?	72
9	Duke	96
10	Forced to Retire	124
11	Panther Pit	133
12	Lenoir Rhyne Returns to Glory	152
13	Monday Morning Quarterback	166
14	The End Zone	176
	Acknowledgments	186

Foreword

It has been said somewhere that, "A coach is only as good as the men his players become." If that is indeed true, then Coach Goldsmith is one of finest ever to grace this profession.

Don't get me wrong; he won a lot games throughout his storied career. He was instrumental in three of the most remarkable turnaround stories in the history of college football. As the defensive coordinator at the Air Force Academy, he oversaw a complete overhaul of the entire program and helped lead them to back to back bowl victories, two consecutive victories over Notre Dame and a final national ranking of #13 his last year there. The job he did as the head coach at Rice and Duke is no less remarkable. He led both programs, historically "whipping boys" for the college football elite, to respectability and prominence. In the case of Duke, he led them to their second bowl game in 34 years in his first year as their head coach. For his efforts, he was rewarded with National and ACC Coach of the Year honors.

I had the great fortune of being a defensive player during his time as Air Force's defensive coordinator. He was not an easy coach to play for because of his undying search for perfection. He knew his defense better than anyone else and how it was supposed to be played. He was way ahead of his time in structuring the eight man front defense which was the precursor to the 4-2-5 defense that is in vogue right now. I had some difficult times during my four years at the Air Force Academy as a cadet and player. There were many days when I wondered if it was worth it to continue and, along with Coach Hatfield and Coach Trott, Coach Goldsmith kept me there. Without those three men, I probably would have taken the easy way out and left like many others. I am grateful that God put him in my life when I really needed him.

I was also blessed to work for Coach Goldsmith as a volunteer coach during his first year as defensive coordinator at The University of Arkansas. As the defensive volunteer coach, I was affectionately called "Fred's boy" because I had played for him at Air Force and he knew me better than the other graduate assistants. As a result of our relationship, he dumped most of the menial tasks on my lap, but I was glad to do them. During that year, Coach and I became closer than we were as player and coach. I got to see him more as a mentor and I am thankful for that. I saw that you could be a good coach without sacrificing as a husband and father. I also learned, during that year, what a good coach is and does and started to develop the work ethic that is required. I stayed up at the office with Coach Goldsmith many nights helping him break down opponents and drawing cards for the next day's practice. He was detailed oriented and his preparation was amazing. One story that demonstrates that is this:

Our regular season had wrapped up and we had already been invited to the 1984 Liberty Bowl. Several teams still had one game left in the regular season and our opponent was yet to be determined. Coach Goldsmith was convinced that we were going to play LSU and had me break down the 10 games that they had already played. He put together a game plan based on that information. Unfortunately for me, we ended up playing Auburn and I had to break down the 11 games that they played so he could develop a game plan for them. What that experience taught me as a young coach is that there is detail in the preparation and that every detail is important. During my short single year as Fred's Boy, I developed many of my coaching philosophies.

My recollections of Coach Goldsmith would be incomplete without mentioning his wife Pam and daughters Kim and Robin. The coaching profession, as great as it is, is extremely stressful on families. It takes a special woman and remarkable kids to share their husband and father with 100 boys. As the saying goes, "Behind any great man is a better woman." In this case, it took three! It was very apparent that Coach G was "Pam's Boy", and she coached him as he did his players! She completed him and helped shape how he related to his fellow coaches and players. Thank God for her, or there is no telling what he would have done with us!

Chuck Petersen USAFA

The First Quarter

I am sure we all wonder what a "real job" would be like! Most coaches that I've known, however, feel blessed never having had to have a real job! I am sure the great recruiters could be good salesmen, but it's more fun to sell a player and his family a college scholarship. Heck, most of us can't change a light bulb. So who are we kidding? We are blessed to make a good living at a "game".

I believe success as a coach comes from being fortunate enough to learn from good people. The kind of people you are exposed to in your career help develop your philosophy and your organization becomes like theirs. I have had the blessing of being exposed to some amazing people throughout my life.

I was born in 1944 in Brooklyn. For the first two years of my childhood, I lived in Brooklyn with my mom, Pearl, Grandpa Max, and my aunts, Esther and Ruth. My grandmother died when Mom was 17. Ruth was a school teacher living at home, and Esther and Pearl lived at home while their husbands were off at war. Esther's husband, Uncle Leo, was an army dentist who survived the Bataan Death March. My maternal grandfather, Dr. Max Goldstein, immigrated to America from Russia in the 1890s. He put himself through medical school. My paternal grandfather, Abe Goldsmith, an immigrant from Austria, was homeless as a boy but learned the fur trade and became very successful.

My family moved to Coral Gables two years after I was born. My mother was a former model, and my father, Phil, was an importer who traveled all over South America and earned a post in Coral Gables, FL because he was bilingual. My parents had grown up catty corner from each other in Brooklyn and married in 1942. Dad had gone to USC and lettered in baseball. He got to know Jackie Robinson playing baseball against him when Jackie played at UCLA. Jackie became my hero. Years later, I wore #42 on my football jersey.

Because my relatives lived within walking distance of Ebbets Field, I became a huge Dodger fan. At age six, I wrote my first fan letter to Jackie Robinson. My uncles used to take my cousins and me to the games. We would wear Dodger uniforms and stand outside the dressing room to get autographs.

Unfortunately, my carefree childhood would come to an end on May 18, 1950. Mom was stricken with polio and would live out the rest of her days in a wheelchair. My brother and I were sent with a nurse to live with Grandpa Max for seven months while Mom was in the hospital. In October 1953, in Coral Gables, I contracted the polio virus. My first night in the hospital I roomed with a little boy who cried all night and a young man in his twenties. When we woke up the next day, the young man had passed away. I found out that Jackie wanted to visit me in the hospital but was not allowed to because of segregation. While I was recuperating, I got a phone call from Jackie. I remember asking him if Pee Wee Reese was going to be the Dodger's new manager.

In December of 1953, the Orange Bowl Shrine Game players came to visit the hospital. An All American quarterback for Michigan State, Earl Morral, visited me. He later played for the Colts and the Dolphins, and we met again playing golf at an ACC function in the late '90s while I was coaching at Duke.

While I was still bedridden with polio, my Grandpa Max flew down to visit me, came into my room, prayed, and told me to get up and try to walk. I walked. By March of 1954, I had recovered enough to watch Jackie and his barnstorming team play in Miami Stadium. It was a little boy's dream to get to see Pee Wee Reese, Gil Hodges, Roy Campanella, Carl Erskine, Don Newcombe and Duke Snider. Jackie was educated and took his role as a leader and role model seriously. Jackie lifted me over the fence and took me into the dressing room with him. He let me sit in the dugout with all the "Boys of Summer". I sat by Jackie and utility outfielder Dick Williams. He was so nice to me. Later he became a Hall of Fame manager with the Boston Red Sox and the Oakland As. It was an unbelievable experience for a ten year old boy.

Overcome with excitement, I starting yelling at the umpire about a call, and Walter Alston said, "Jackie, you'd better control that kid!"

In 1956, I was playing baseball as an All Star shortstop for the Southwest Boys Club little league team. Bob Graham, my baseball coach, talked me into going out for his 109 lb. and under football team. Tall and skinny, about 5'6''in the seventh grade, I was told I would be another Don Hutson. Hutson was an all pro receiver for the Green Bay Packers. I had never heard of him, but I wound up playing anyway. The team went undefeated in the fall and won the Intercity Athletic Conference. We got to play a Coral Gables All Star team in the Junior Orange Bowl. We lost, but I caught a three yard touchdown pass. I did great until it got dark, and then I couldn't see without my glasses. The next year, I was one of the few eighth graders on an unlimited weight football team made up of eight and ninth graders.

My coach was a fireman named Joe Atwood. Joe was a father figure to me since my Dad was always traveling; he was the one who inspired me to become a coach. Our team never lost a game against our own age division. Our only loss came against powerhouse Miami High's JV team, and it was close, 6-0.

Academically, eighth grade was a rough year. I hated math and was getting bad grades and skipping school. When Dad showed up at school, I was in even more trouble because he caught me sleeping in math class. I couldn't play in the last two games and got a whipping at home and a paddling at school. This early experience stayed with me, and throughout my coaching career I always checked in with teachers and called parents of players who were skipping class.

During ninth grade I was able to rejoin the team. We had a successful year and many of my ninth grade teammates earned major college scholarships. One player played for Florida, one went to the University of Pennsylvania, one went to Wichita State, one went to the University of Tampa, one played for Miami, two played for Georgia, one played at Florida State, and two played for Georgia Tech. We even had an All American.

High School

In 1959, I was excited about playing for Coral Gables High School. They had won the state championship when I was in seventh and ninth grade. That was before the Miami Dolphins, and 25,000 to 50,000 people would come to the Orange Bowl to watch high school games. Coral Gables would also travel by train and play Jacksonville teams in the Gator Bowl.

My tenth grade year, I played on the JV football team. Jack Card, the greatest friend anybody could have, played sports with me at the Boys' Club. Two other teammates, Bill Klich and John Douglas were my neighbors. When we experienced our first challenging high school two a day practices together, I was thankful that Mrs. Klich brought us all Absorbine Jr. to use between practices.

Even though baseball was my favorite sport, I never played again after losing out to Woody Woodward for the short stop position on the Coral Gables HS team. Woody went on to be the short stop for the Atlanta Braves and the Big Red Machine.

In 1960, my junior year, we only lost one football game. We lost to Jacksonville Lee and tied Miami High 13-13. Some of the guys, including our kicker, Robbie Hasencamp, were in 7-Eleven together the day after the tie game. I felt terrible for Robbie when the clerk told us it was too bad the kicker had missed the field goal.

In our senior year, 1961, Gables would have another great year marred only by a loss to Miami Edison and a 0-0 tie with Miami High. Gables head coach Nick Kotys had been well coached at Villanova by Harry Stuhldreher, one of Knute Rockne's four horsemen at Notre Dame. My position coach, Joe Krutulis, played at Miami. He was like a dad to me. Ed Injaychock was the offensive line coach, Jack McCloskey was the defensive coordinator, and Sam Scarnechia was the new defensive back coach. Sam was a yeller, but Coach Krutulis told him, "Take it easy Sam, these boys are good." We were good. Nick was a great coach who only averaged 1.5 losses a year for 31 years of high school coaching. I respected all my coaches, and Scarnechia made an impression on me when he shook hands with every senior at the end of the last game. It was a tradition I would incorporate when I became a head coach. Ed and Jack kept up with me over the years, and I brought them in to talk to our Duke and Franklin teams.

In addition to solid coaching, Gables had incredible talent. Some of the standout players that were highly recruited by Division I schools my senior year included: Jim Mansene, Mike Brady, John

Douglas, Larry Blume, Ron Pantello, Joel Goldman, and Steve Clifford. Jack Card was a phenomenal athlete. At 5'8" 167 lbs., he went on to be a starting linebacker at Florida and start in the Sugar Bowl and Orange Bowl.

1961 was a life changing year for me. It was the year I began two relationships that would change the rest of my life. During that year I met Jesus Christ and my wife, Pam Penland. Robbie Hasencamp came from a strong Christian family. I enjoyed being around them, especially his older sister, Judy, who I had a little crush on. When Robbie invited the guys to a Billy Graham Crusade, Jack and I went all week, and on March 13, 1961, I went forward to ask Jesus Christ to forgive my sins and be my Lord and Savior. I prayed with Grady Wilson, and Mr. Hasencamp gave me a Bible. I read it from cover to cover over the next several weeks. When I told my Jewish mother about my decision to become a Christian, there was tension at home, and I ended up staying with Jack Card until she calmed down. University Baptist Church taught me about my new faith. T. Rupert Coleman was our pastor, and he explained that people could have personal relationships with God. I was baptized and joined his church. My Sunday school teacher was Jack Bracington. Jack had played football for the University of Miami and he was an excellent role model.

Later in 1961, when I was a high school senior, I saw my wife, Pam Penland, at a pep rally the night before Thanksgiving. She was only a ninth grader, and I was aggravated because all my friends were talking to her, and I was in a hurry. I said, "Why are ya'll talking to that ninth grader?" Even though she was only 15, Pam was beautiful; it was easy to see why there was a crowd of boys around her. On December 29, 1961, I was introduced to her at the Junior Orange Bowl parade. That night I had a chance to dance with her at the Coral Gables Country Club.

On Good Friday in 1962, I was supposed to have a date with another girl, but she got mono and I asked Pam to go with me to a dance. She had to ask her mother who was sitting in the carpool line picking her up from school. On Easter Sunday we went to the Passion Play in the Orange Bowl. When I picked Pam up, her dad asked about my college aspirations. I told him I had a football scholarship to Western Carolina; that won points with Bob. His brother Farrell had been on Western's first football team.

College

My recruiting experience was a little bit different than that of my teammates who were pursued by major colleges. An English teacher from Asheville, Mrs. Callahan, told me about Western Carolina. Then my coach sent them film, and they invited me to attend a recruiting weekend on April 13-14, 1962. When I saw my buddies getting plane tickets from schools like Duke and Georgia, I called the college to find out why my plane ticket hadn't arrived. He tactfully explained that they wouldn't be providing a plane ticket to North Carolina.

I signed with Western Carolina, but I would not play football for long. I was 12 hours away from home, homesick, and injured after starting in an early game against Catawba. At the end of the first semester, I took my history final earlier than the other students. History was my best subject, and I knew I had an A going into the final. However, when the grades came in the mail, I discovered an F on my report card. The professor had failed me because some football players who had taken the test later got As. He accused me of cheating by giving them the answers, and I flunked out of school. I had no way to prove my innocence and finished that year at the University of Miami in the spring of 1963. I returned to Western for the 1963-64 season and had to play on the scout team because I was still considered academically ineligible. I got out of shape and decided that without football panning out, Western wasn't really the school for me.

In the summer of 1964, I went back to Miami and worked for Pam's dad, Bob Penland. Bob owned the KoolKraft air conditioning company in Miami. It was so hot putting insulation in attics that I lost 15 lbs. in a week. I also fell through a client's ceiling into a group of ladies playing bridge, and Bob had to replace the whole living room ceiling. I know Bob would have fired me if I hadn't been dating his daughter. It sure inspired me to go into coaching.

After a visit to Jack Card at the University of Florida, I enjoyed the atmosphere on campus so much that I decided to transfer there. I went home to Miami Dade Junior College to get my grades up and coached the JV team at Coral Gables High School part-time They won another state championship that year. In January of 1965, I became a student at the University of Florida. I pledged Sigma Nu and worked in our dining room cooking and serving breakfast to help pay my way. Jack and Kathleen Card helped out by inviting me over for suppers, but I still needed to find a coaching job to pay the bills.

High School Coaching Jobs

I had helped Larry Travis, one of the Gator coaches, when he was recruiting Larry Rentz, the quarterback for Coral Gables' 1964 championship team. Travis returned the favor by arranging an interview with Jim Niblack, the Gainesville High School head coach. Even though the pay for the assistant coaching position was only $300.00 a year, the experience coaching tight ends and defensive ends was invaluable.

Gainesville High's 1965 team was loaded with talent. We had Kim Helton, who would later coach against me when I was the head coach at Rice and he was the head coach at Houston, Jackie Eckdahl and Brian Hipp played for Florida, Tommy Hanson started at Richmond, Allen Speer went to Vanderbilt, Eugene Branch played for Auburn, John Wayne Jackson went to Memphis State, and Bobby Rountree started at the AFA. Gainesville was a prestigious program with experienced coaches. Jim Niblack later coached at Kentucky and for the Buffalo Bills. Wesley Dicks was the directing teacher that I student taught under. He was also a successful high school coach at Gainesville who would later take them to the state championship as a head coach. Hurley Manning went on to establish a winning tradition as head coach at Milton Florida High School. Robert Davis became a legend at Warner Robbins HS and Loren Giannamore did well at Vero Beach HS in Florida. Jack Jones later became a successful coach at Santa Fe and joined the staff at the University of Florida.

The rookie coaches were: Gene Roberts, Fritchie Smith, me, and Garney Hatch. Garney was also our head basketball coach. Because of that, he discovered Eddie McAshan on the basketball team. Eddie was an incredibly talented ambidextrous athlete and our first black football player. Niblack took some heat from his family and the community but didn't back down. Eddie became the first in a long line of black athletes to play for Gainesville and advance to the college ranks.

I learned tremendous work habits from Niblack's staff. Even in the off season, we were working hard and bringing in college coaches to teach us new schemes. We also had an advantage most teams didn't have yet. Dr. Cade was just starting to make Gatorade in the lab at the University of Florida, and Jack Card's wife Kathleen was Dr. Cade's secretary. She would send Gatorade to Gainesville HS in old Clorox bottles.

On June 11, 1966 Pam and I married. She got food poisoning on our honeymoon and got so sick that we had to move in with her parents for a few days. When we finally moved into a garage apartment in Gainesville, I was worried that the $85.00 a month rent was too high to handle on my $75.00 a month salary. Fortunately, Pam got a job at the school board office. Our first home was so small that I could stand in the shower and brush my teeth in the sink at the same time. We had to leave the trash in the kitchen sink to keep the roaches away. When we moved into that little apartment, we packed all of our belongings in trash bags instead of boxes. As we started unpacking, I realized I had accidentally thrown all of Pam's shoes away.

Steve and Jerri Spurrier were friends from the University of Florida, and they knew that we had thought about eloping and found a place to get married, so they asked us to go with them when they decided to get married in September. I got a little confused on the directions and instead of going to Folkston, GA, we got lost and ended up in Kingsland, GA. Steve and I were both rushing back for football practice, and Steve got a speeding ticket on the way back. After that ticket, Spurrier may have slowed down when he was driving, but he didn't slow down on the field. He won the Heisman trophy that November.

In 1967, I planned on teaching history and continuing to coach at Gainesville HS, but Spurgeon Cherry, a professor at the University of Florida, told me to interview with Harry T. Reid. Harry was the

Hamilton High School superintendent of schools. Cherry had been one of the most successful high school football coaches in the country. He said, "Fred Goldsmith, if you don't take that job, you don't have the guts to find out what you can do on your own." I was only 23 so I thought it would be a long shot for me to get a head coaching job, but I went ahead and interviewed with the Board of Trustees. It helped that the Chairman of the Board, Dr. Fred Mickler, knew my friend Larry Rentz. Dr. Mickler's son was going to be the quarterback, and it was a brand new school. I was excited, but Pam loved Gainesville and wasn't anxious to move. When I finished the interview, she said, "I'm sure glad that's over. I can't wait to get home!" I told her, "Honey, I told them I'd take the job." I got the job the week I graduated from the University of Florida.

Pam felt better about it when I bought her a house on her twentieth birthday. Since both our birthdays were the same week in March, Pam splurged and bought me my first pair of nice coaching shoes. We soon found out we were expecting our first child. Dr. Mickler would deliver our daughter Kim on December 8, 1967. We liked Jasper and had friendly neighbors who took us in and brought us meals. It was a small town where people never locked their doors, and everyone rooted for the home team.

Hamilton High's record was 2-8 when I took over, and we went 4-5-1 that year. I had learned from two veteran head coaches who were established and successful and tried to emulate them, but now I realize that I should have taken the time to earn respect instead of making demands as a new coach. Later on, I learned to be more diplomatic and pick my battles. My inexperience contributed to a humbling homecoming loss that year. Hamilton County High was up 6-0 with just seconds to go, and I neglected to tell my quarterback to take a knee rather than run a play. As a result, we fumbled and Joey Shonicker returned the fumble 30 yards for a touchdown for Dixie County High School. They won the game and the conference championship.

The most exciting win that year was a huge upset over Doyle McCall's Chiefland HS team. Their best player was a huge, fast running back named Willie Givens. He was one of the first black players in the Sewanee conference and Hamilton had to play great defense to contain him.

In 1968, I headed back to Miami for a short stint as the head JV coach and history teacher at a larger school, Coral Park HS. It was an opportunity to work for Frank Downing. My most vivid memory from that year occurred off the field when a student gave me a fifth of vodka with the top loosened for a Christmas present. I was a floating teacher who didn't have my own room, so I had to stick it in my briefcase. When I got to the next class, it had spilled all over my papers. The students were roaring and the department head, a former Lieutenant Commander in the Navy, was furious. She didn't like me when I was in her world history class at Gables High several years before, and she still didn't like me when I taught at her school.

In 1969, I decided I wanted to be a head coach again and applied for the job at Charlotte HS in Port Charlotte FL. They had only won five games in the previous eight years. That first year, we went 6-4. The second year we won 10 games.

How many guys in a small high school have players like Burton Lawless? Burton had become a Christian through the high school FCA program. He was an unbelievable athlete with character. Before Lawless, the program had not sent anyone to a Division I college. During the 1969-1970 winning seasons, Charlotte High had many highly recruited players. The most successful one was tight end and linebacker Burton Lawless. Everyone wanted Burton. Bear Bryant recruited him along with Florida State, Penn State, and Auburn. He played for Florida and later was the only rookie from the 1975 NFL draft to start for the Cowboys in Super Bowl XII. Harold Mack was a running back who became the all time leading rusher at CHS and attended Florida State. Boo Boo Weaver was a quarterback and all state linebacker who went to Bethel College. The team had great chemistry and talented assistant coaches in Mike Lay, Dave Lawrence, Mike Eader, Gary Rapp and Jack Card.

Wayne Sallade, Chairman of the 2010 Hall of Fame Committee at Charlotte H.S. said:

> Goldsmith changed the culture of the football mindset in this community. Now it is one of the programs recognized in Southwest Florida football, and that traces back to '69 and '70. He

made us believe in ourselves that we were not inferior and could play with anybody.

One of my best memories of those years is helping out when Joe Paterno brought Penn State to the Orange Bowl in 1969 and 1970. The Orange Bowl Committee appointed me to chauffeur Paterno. I also subbed as a quarterback on their scout team. I had a good time except for losing my wedding ring taking snaps. Fortunately, Penn State coach Frank Patrick found it.

Coach Paterno remembered, "He was right there all the time. He even changed a few diapers, babysat for us, and drove Sue to mass." I always wanted to coach for Joe Pa. Early in my career, I heard about an opening and decided to show Coach Paterno how badly I wanted the job. Pam and I used the money in our savings to buy a plane ticket, and I showed up at his office only to discover that he was out of town. His secretary took pity on me and contacted him. When Coach Paterno found out and called me, he said, "Freddie, that's the dumbest thing I've ever heard of!" However, he later told my daughter, "I wish I had been able to hire him at the time. He's a heck of a guy and a heck of a coach, and a real credit to his profession." I never worked for him, but we stayed in touch. When my brother was in a nursing home one of his friends, an 85 year old lifelong Penn State season ticket holder, was terrified about having surgery. David knew she was a huge fan and asked me to call Coach Paterno and have him talk to her. I hated to bug him again because I had just asked him to send a picture for her birthday a few months earlier. He called and of course she was thrilled to hear from him. That's the Joe Paterno I remember.

In January of 1971, Bill Petersen, a former Florida State coach, got the head job at Rice and wanted to hire me as a grad assistant. Little did I know when I met the new secretary at Rice, Barbara Tolar, that she would be my secretary when I returned as the head coach 18 years later. The coaching convention happened to be in Houston that year, and I mentioned the interview to Coach Doug Dickey. Coach Dickey asked me to come to work for him as a graduate assistant with the Gators instead. I jumped at the chance to work with Dickey, a product of Frank Broyles, who was a product of Bobby Dodd. He said he would pay me $666.00 a quarter and give me football tickets.

At this point, I had a family to support, so I called Tommy Tomlinson at the school board office to see if Pam could get her old job back, and we called Pam's widowed grandmother to see if she would be willing to move in to take care of Kim. Ken Hatfield was the secondary coach and the only coach in the office when I reported for duty. Ken had played for Coach Dickey at Arkansas and had coached with him at Tennessee. I also worked with Doug Knotts, who would later be an administrative assistant for me at Duke, Lindy Infanty, our running back coach, became the head football coach of the Green Bay Packers and an NFL Coach of the Year, and Bill Carr, another graduate assistant, would become the youngest athletic director at the University of Florida at age 34.

Duke beat the Gators in the first game, and we lost the next four. Going into the sixth game, I was in charge of scouting Florida State. Coach Dickey sent me to represent him at the press conference. Florida State had only beaten UF once in 20 years, but this year UF was 0-5 and FSU was 5-0 going into the game. When a reporter asked if UF had a chance, I replied, "Of course we have a chance, we're UF and they're FSU. We don't expect to do anything but win." Coach Dickey was upset because this went out on the air and got FSU fired up. Fortunately for me, we won 17-15. Florida State threw a pass and it was ruled out of bounds. If FSU had been in, they would have kicked and won the game. Hatfield and Knotts had come up with a good defensive strategy - five underneath man with a two deep zone combo coverage. Florida suffered their worst season in 20 years, but I gained valuable experience.

My next job, in 1972, was at Deland High School. I inherited a 0-10 team that was about to enter its first year in the Big 8 conference, the toughest conference in Florida. When we moved, I sold my old car and got a bike. When our tight end, Blain Owen, moved into the area, his dad was a car dealer, so he let me use the driver's education car to get to and from work. One day after a dismal spring practice, I decided to take my family to Disney World. It had just opened and we paid six dollars for each ticket. I'm not sure

who had the best time, my five year old, or Pam's 78
year old grandmother.

There were several keys to turning the program
around. Deland hired me immediately before spring
practice, and I didn't have any teaching duties until the
following year, so I could focus solely on football. Our
supporters included Terry Acree, who organized the
Deland H.S. improvement fund to support the football
program, and Red Calkins, whose son Frank played on
the team. The locker room was atrocious, so Red
raised money for a new locker room. Roger Gilmore,
the local sports editor, publicized a spaghetti supper at
the Catholic church. The players, their fathers, and
other members of the community came together and
built the building in one day. The shop teacher donated
new lockers and the effort brought together a
community divided by racial tension. At a preseason
jamboree, I discovered a star in Marion Jeffries. He
was only 140 lbs., but he burst on the scene. When he
became a father, the players raised money to feed the
baby. Another factor was weight training. Arthur Jones
invented Nautilus and had his weight room in a
building behind the school. These machines were a
novelty, so even the Japanese government came to find
out about them. Pros including Dick Butkus, Coach
Don Shula, and Pete Brown, the owner of the Bengals,
all came down and tried them out. They were the first
to buy the equipment for their NFL franchises. Deland
H.S. had access to the equipment and started a weight
lifting class, so we were able to become stronger than
the competition.

I had a dedicated and capable staff. Les Valerie had been the head coach at a local black school that had been phased out with integration, so he brought experience and helped the school through the transition. JV coach Tony Tussing was a hard worker who drove an hour and a half to process the game film and deposit it on my doorstep. I was also able to hire David Hiss, a talented young coach who would spend 10 years as Deland's head coach. Hiss started a wrestling program with one heavyweight wrestler, a 6' 250 lb. lineman named Tim Chavers. Since Chavers didn't have anyone to wrestle with, Hiss had to wrestle him every day so he could practice.

Deland had better prospects for 1972. We had a good QB in Glen Goodwin and Billy Brown was a great fullback. Tyrone Tinsley was an effective safety and punter, even though he punted with the end of his toe. Tim Chavers did well and became a starter at defensive tackle at FAMU. The first game was against Jacksonville Wolfson. We were tied 0-0 until the last few minutes, and then Audie Murphy caught a touchdown pass at the end of the game. The 1972 season ended with a 5-5-1 record and an appearance in the Christmas Bowl. We played Gainesville East Side.

Rabbit Smith was Gainesville East Side's coach. I had gone to Coach Smith for defensive advice several years earlier when he was coaching at Florida. Coach Smith had taught me an eight man front wide tackle six defense and we had implemented it at Hamilton HS and run it ever since. It was no surprise that the game ended in a 0-0 tie. At the end of that season, our daughter Robin was born on December 27, 1972.

In 1973, we had more talent with a championship junior high team moving up, but two of the best backs, Fred Betsy and Sanford Cutts, eventually dropped out of school. They would have definitely had a future in college football if they had stayed. In our season opener, Deland played Jacksonville Wolfson in the Gator Bowl. I had gone over to the University of Tennessee the summer before and picked up a play action pass from their coaches. We were able to use that to score a long touchdown in the first series of the game. We had to come from behind in the second game against Leesburg. Behind 7-6 with a minute to go, Leesburg snapped the ball before the quarterback was ready, and they fumbled. Deland got to the 50 on the next play, and we called a timeout to put in the 134 box play we had used at Gables. I knew the other team might be looking, so we pointed to the receivers to go wide and deep while Betsy delayed and went down the middle for a short pass. The receivers dropped back for a fake and Leesburg double covered them. Goodwin threw a 50 yard pass to Betsy for a touchdown to win. Most of the fans were on their way home and heard it on the radio. We played the Sanford Seminoles in our last game. They had a player named Tim Raines that could fly. He later played for the Yankees. The season ended with a 14-14 tie. Deland would also beat Daytona Mainland and Dayton Sea Breeze. Our record was 5-4-1.

I'm So Glad I'm From FAMU

In 1974, spring practice was going well and Deland had a winning attitude. Out of the blue, Lambert Reed, a defensive line coach for Florida, came to see me. He had interviewed for the Florida A&M University job and needed a minority linebacker coach at the historically black university. I knew they had a great tradition and Jake Gaither, their legendary coach, had spoken at Deland's football banquet that year. When Reed didn't get the job, I was disappointed. Matthew Fair, Deland's assistant principal, encouraged me to contact the new head coach, Rudy Hubbard. Hubbard had been an assistant under Woody Hayes at Ohio State, and I assumed he would hire bigger names. Hubbard agreed to interview me for defensive coordinator. I stayed up most of the night studying Ken Hatfield's playbook from Florida. The Gators' defense was similar to Ohio State's and I thought it would give me an advantage. I drove three hours to Tallahassee and interviewed for 13 hours straight. I got home so tired that I couldn't even remember Rudy's name.

Rudy offered me the job and I was thrilled to accept it and move to the college ranks. I was the only white coach at the school. It was a bit of an adjustment for Pam. At her first wives' get together, the ladies turned on the music and taught her a popular 70s dance, The Bump. Even though they were conspicuous as the only white people in the stands, my family enjoyed the atmosphere. Sometimes if the game was well in hand, I would take my daughter Kim down to the field at halftime and put her on my shoulders to watch the band perform.

Rudy Hubbard had coached and played under Woody Hayes and Hayes had learned from Paul Brown, so Rudy knew how to run a tight ship. He followed Woody's example in doing room checks to make sure students were studying. He wanted a strong recruiting coach who would be able to attract good students. Hubbard also changed academic expectations at FAMU. It was a Division II school and many of the players were players that didn't have the grades for Division I schools. If guys couldn't cut it academically, they usually had more trouble understanding plays, so Rudy decided to recruit better students. He even required players to read poetry aloud after practice because he wanted his players to use proper diction when they were interviewed by the media.

Coach Hubbard didn't put up with bad behavior. The Orange Blossom Classic was always the last game of the season. When he found out that players traditionally hazed the freshmen after the last practice before that game, he ordered them to stop because they were running off recruits. He told them if he found out they were hazing, he would put them off the team. Five or six of them went ahead and did it. Some of them were starters. Rudy found out that a starting linebacker was threatening not to play without his friends. Now no one got on the bus after Rudy did. He called that player and said, "You've got about 10 minutes. I'm leaving these guys here and if you don't get on the bus in 10 minutes, you've had a good year and I'll see you later." On the bus ride, Hubbard found out there were five or six more guys involved. He called their parents to come get them. We won with no backups, and that experience helped FAMU go into the next year undefeated because so many young guys saw their first playing time during the Classic. With that kind of discipline in place, the school had a good reputation in the community.

I served as the recruiting coordinator and defensive coordinator. My connections with south Florida high school coaches helped us recruit some good players. I recruited Marvin Fair, Tim Chavers, and Jeff and Frank Grady from Deland. Jeff went on to start for the Giants. I also recruited Harold Oliver from Hamilton High School in Jasper. He went on to be an All American at FAMU.

The biggest success we had in recruiting came in 1976. The day after the Orange Blossom Classic, a coach from Miami Killian, Don Soldinger, called me about Gifford "Spanky" Ramsey. He was a strong safety and looked great on film. Bear Bryant happened to be speaking at his football banquet after I signed him. Bear decided he wanted him when he saw the highlight film, but he said he would not take him because Jake Gaither, our athletic director emeritus, was one of his good friends, and he wouldn't take a player away from FAMU. One of FAMU's players, Curtis Parnell, who played the same position, student taught at Spanky's school and taught Spanky the position before he ever reported. Spanky intercepted a pass for a touchdown in his first college start against Alcorn State as a true freshman.

In addition to being tough on the players, Hubbard demanded excellence from his coaches. Rudy admitted he was a tough boss. He had the coaches put on clinics for the staff to prove that we knew what we were talking about. If it didn't make sense to the other coaches, it wouldn't make sense to the players. Many coaches didn't like that, but Allen Bogan and I saw the value of it and embraced it. Rudy always used to ask me before a game, "How many points do you expect they will score?" I didn't like that question. I didn't know what to say. He wanted me to say none. In 1976, FAMU had been badly beaten by Bethune Cookman. Rudy recalled, "I told the alumni after that if we didn't have a great year, I would resign. I looked at Fred, and he had the most disgusted look on his face! He probably thought I shouldn't have said it publicly, but I knew we had a heck of a squad coming back."

Bethune Cookman was FAMU's biggest rivalry. That first year Hubbard took over, 1974, we played them in the Daytona Beach Speedway. The race track was filled with sand spurs since it was so close to the beach. It was an embarrassing 6-0 loss. In 1975,

Bethune Cookman was undefeated at 10-0 and FAMU was 8-2. The game was played in Doak Campbell Stadium in front of 40,000 fans. Their coach said they were too good to play FAMU and should have been playing FSU. FAMU rose to the challenge. Jeff Grady sacked them for a 30 yard loss. Curtis "Pecan" Parnell also had some great plays. FAMU was ahead 10-7 and Pecan intercepted a pass and ran it back for a TD. He was swarmed by the FAMU crowd and came out with a helmet full of $20 bills.

In 1977, FAMU became the nation's only undefeated and untied team and won the Black College National Championship. Texas was the only other team that was undefeated at the end of that season, but they lost their bowl game. Woody Hayes had said it took four or five years to build a program from scratch; that proved true everywhere I coached. By that time, FAMU was outdrawing Miami with 30,000 plus fans attending the Orange Blossom Classic. I was happy at FAMU, but when I found out about an opening at Florida State, I decided to apply for the position. Rudy Hubbard and Doug Dickey called and recommended me for the job. Coach Bowden called me in for an interview, but we had never met in person. When he saw me, he laughed and called me back into his office. He told me he had a position open for a black coach and had assumed I was a black coach because I was at FAMU.

Tallahassee had been our home for five years. Pam worked for Landmark Realty, and we had settled down at Faith Presbyterian Church where I was a deacon, and we were in a couple's Bible study. We liked the area so much that in 1978 I got out of coaching to go into business, and the plan was to stay in Tallahassee for the rest of our lives. We had even convinced Pam's parents to move there. We were looking forward to a sane schedule and normal life and bought season tickets for FSU's football games. But I missed the game too much and started having second thoughts at a deacons' retreat. Bill Crutchfield, a fellow deacon, had given Bo Schembeckler his first job when Bill was the head coach at Presbyterian College. I respected his opinion. Crutchfield told me that he missed having the podium to share Christ as a Christian coach. After a few months, I returned to football.

In 1978, FAMU became the last team admitted to Division IAA and beat the University of Massachusetts to win a national championship in Wichita Falls, KS. We led the nation in rushing, scoring, and total defense. FAMU would beat Miami 16-13 in 1979, but I wouldn't be around to see it.

Off We Go
Into the Wild Blue Yonder

In 1979, Ken Hatfield, my friend from the
University of Florida, succeeded Bill Parcells as the
head coach at the USAFA and offered me a job at
12:30a.m. I took it without consulting Pam. I said yes
because Pam had always said she wanted to go to
Colorado. I hung up the phone, turned to Pam, and
asked if she was awake. I said, "Did Ken Hatfield just
call me?" (I always dreamt about job offers, so I
thought I might have been dreaming.) Pam said yes.
Then I said, "I guess we're moving to Colorado." Pam
said, "What?" I said, "You said you always wanted to
go there." She replied, "I meant on vacation." This
should be a lesson to young coaches to discuss
decisions with their wives. Pam soon got over the
shock, and we were both excited about the move to
Colorado. The hardest part of leaving was telling
Pam's parents. I was heartbroken when I had to go tell
my father-in-law that we were moving, and I saw him
walking along holding hands with my girls.

Hatfield said I was his first hire. Ken became a
lifelong friend who taught me what it meant to live the

Christian life by serving and caring for others. He assembled an experienced staff that worked well together: Al Groh was the first defensive coordinator and later became the head coach of the New York Jets, Buffalo Bills head coach and former Dallas Cowboys head coach Chan Gailey was the secondary coach first before he became the defensive coordinator, Tom Backhus went to Notre Dame after our first two years, Billy Mitchell was a military coach, and Bobby Trott went on to coach in the pros for ten years. Later Ken would hire Fisher DeBerry, Larry Beckman, Wally Ake, Jim Goodman, and Mike Heimerdinger.

The staff would become close; many of our careers ended up intersecting decades later. We worked hard and took our responsibilities seriously. DeBerry says:

> We knew we were in coaching to help them be better men and better Christians. We felt it was our ministry. We had a good offensive and defensive system people were not familiar with at that time. We had quality people and a family atmosphere. In the Bible, I Sam 2:30 says, 'I will honor those who honor me.' Ken built the program under that premise. The players knew we cared about each other. There was love and respect among the players and coaches. We had a commitment to football and a vision. As we won two, four, eight, and finally 10 games under Hatfield, God honored our efforts in trying to do His work through football.

The coaches learned from each other and challenged each other. We did a Bible study every Thursday. Chan challenged me to clean up my language with the players. Ken discouraged profanity as well. I didn't always succeed, but I tried. Shawn Smith remembers that I used to say, "Aw, Sugar, Shawn Smith!" or call him the Guthrie Goat (he was from Guthrie, OK) whenever I would get upset over a bad read in practice. Once, after Hatfield lost his temper and cussed during the CSU game, he decided to give the players Sunday afternoon off and just show the film on Monday instead of practicing. Coach Hatfield apologized to the team and explained that we shouldn't be out there if we couldn't talk nicely to each other. We went on to win the Commander in Chief trophy, beat Notre Dame, and go to a bowl. We kept winning and decided to keep the same schedule for the rest of season. We continued it at Arkansas. The Razorback fans doubted that we could win giving the players a day off every week, but we proved them wrong and Ken Hatfield still has the highest winning percentage of any coach at the U of A. Eventually the NCAA made it a rule for every school give the players a day off every week.

General O. Sampson was our FCA sponsor. He told us that he noticed how Ken's staff shared a commitment to Christ and that was evident in the way we interacted with each other and the cadets.

That faith was tested in December 1982 when one of our players, Derek Foster, had a wreck on the ice. He was in a coma and expected to die. Mrs. Foster didn't give up, and she and Sandy Hatfield prayed and talked to him for months. In March, Hatfield, Ake, Trott, and I heard he was being transferred to a hospital in New York to be closer to home. Before they put him on a military aircraft, we all prayed and laid hands on him. Derek seemed extremely restless that morning. At 3:00p.m., he came out of the coma. It was a thrill to see him walk out on the field and participate in the coin toss as an honorary captain for the BYU game the next year.

The staff worked hard, but we also played hard. Jim Goodman said, "I had the best time with them. Coaching is about the people you are with. There is no profession like it with that kind of camaraderie and that's the truth." He tells a story about a racquetball game that we played:

> You know how coaches gig each other. Someone got to teasing Fred about being an athlete and he said, 'Goodman, I can whip you in anything.' I was 29 and he was 37 and Chan Gailey used to play both of us in racquetball because we couldn't beat him by ourselves. Well we had an old racquetball court downstairs at the Academy. You had to go down a tunnel under the road about 400 yards. I won the first game and Fred was ahead in the second game when he charged the ball. I heard something pop and Fred started hoppin' on one foot and yelling, 'Did you hit me?' He had torn his Achilles tendon. I ran all the way upstairs, found Chan, and we ran down. Chan said,

'We've got to make a carrying chair.' So we carried him upstairs in the old Boy Scout hold, and we get all the way upstairs and find out there's a wheelchair by an elevator.

It happened so fast that none of us remembered there was an elevator. Goodman didn't feel too sorry for me though. I still had my cast on while we were playing golf, and he hit a curve too fast and slung me out of the golf cart.

The players had a good time too. The upperclassmen would haze the freshmen when they went on their first road trips with the team. They would get a waiter to ask for the team's attention and then announce that one of the freshmen had a phone call. This was a big deal at the Academy back then because there were no cell phones and freshmen cadets were rarely allowed to call home. When the cadet came back in, all the other players would laugh at them. The players also had talent shows and did imitations of the coaches. Jeff Hays did me, and a manager nicknamed Tattoo could imitate everyone and had us rolling before a big Army game. It broke the tension and kept us loose.

The wives were close as well and would get together and listen to the games under the Aspen trees in a local park. We all lived within walking distance of each other in base housing, and the children could walk to school. It was a wonderful experience for our families. Most of us had come from the South, and we enjoyed snow days, sledding on the practice field, ice

skating, skiing, horseback riding, hiking Pike's Peak
and the Garden of the Gods, visiting Aspen, going to
the Flying W Ranch, and rodeos. We also took our
wives to Hawaii to play the University of Hawaii. It
was a somber experience, though, when we visited
Pearl Harbor and could still see the oil from the U.S.S.
Arizona.

Pam started a ministry in downtown Colorado
Springs that fed the poor and shared the gospel. As we
moved around with each college coaching job, Pam
was able to start this ministry in each new city. When
she held a 5K run as a fundraiser, astronaut Jim Irwin
ran in the race and spoke at our FCA share time. As we
moved all over the country, I believe God used Pam's
ministry to make a difference and change lives
everywhere we lived.

Coaching at the Academy provided some
interesting experiences that coaches don't normally get
to try. Graduation ceremonies at the Academy were
impressive; many times the commencement speaker
was the president or vice president.

I had the opportunity to attend the Operation
Red Flag war games at Nellis Air Force Base and get
to sit in a simulator at NASA the day before a launch.
The staff also got to meet the Thunderbirds and go up
in F-16s. Some of the military personnel that I came to
respect during this time were: Colonel John Clune, our
AD, Superintendent General Ken Tallman, and
General Dick Abel, who was stationed at the Pentagon.
Gen. Abel was a Christian who had flown the first

POWs out of Vietnam and counseled them on the way home. He was a great motivational speaker for the cadets and would do the FCA team share times. Later he became the FCA president. Clebe McClary, a Vietnam vet and football coach would also visit Ken Hatfield and speak to our team. In later years Clebe became a great friend and spoke to our Arkansas, Rice, Duke, and LR football team. Col. Roy Smith was an Air Force reserve officer and admissions counselor for students interested in the AFA. In 1979 he was the area athletic coordinator serving as a liason between the Texas high school coaches, our recruits and their parents, and the AFA coaches.

Recruiting for the USAFA was more challenging than recruiting for other colleges. The student athletes had to have high SAT or ACT scores and be in top physical shape to handle the military requirements. It was hard for football players to do pull ups and the players couldn't be bigger than 6'5" and 260 lbs because they had to fit into the planes. The biggest obstacle to getting recruits was that they had to commit to five years in the military after graduation. Some of them made it to the Academy only to drop out during basic training.

However, there were some advantages to recruiting for the AFA. People across the nation had a respect for the Academy, so recruiting was national, and in some cases, international. For highly motivated students who had a desire to lead the country, the best place to learn leadership would be on the football field at a service academy. All cadets also received a monthly stipend of $480.00 in addition to a free education.

When Hatfield and I teamed up with Col. Smith to recruit in Houston, we were stepping into one of the most fertile areas for high school prospects in the country. Texas was strong in academics, conservative, and patriotic. In Texas, we found smaller players who were not national All Americans, but they were smart, competitive kids who could understand the wishbone and had a strong work ethic. They had the grades to go to the Academy, but they were undersized. My definition of an ideal player was one who ran fast, had a "we not me" attitude, and played with intensity. Some of our early recruits who became strong contributors to the success of the program were: Charlie Heath, Jeff Hays, Kelly Pittman, Jerry Rose, and future All American Mike Kirby. Ted Sundquist, one of our first recruits, and former general manager of the Denver Broncos said:

> Dignified in his uniform, Colonel Smith painted a fantastic picture of what a future in the military could mean to us. Coach Goldsmith answered every question I had and impressed me by coming to see me receive awards. He made all of us feel wanted. To this day, thirty years later, he still asks about my mom.

Col. Smith says the worst part of recruiting was driving with me. He thought I drove too slowly in Houston traffic, and Hatfield thought I was too fast.

Col. Smith recalls, "He hated entering the freeway and would come to a dead stop instead of merging. I started picking him up at the airport instead of letting him rent a car." Hatfield agreed, "Fred was the worst driver on our staff. Driving with Fred was like flying in a twin engine plane with one engine out. Fred would drive and talk as I watched for the exit. One time I yelled to Fred that the exit was now- only to have him swerve over five lanes as cars dodged us and drivers yelled at us. Fred was an adventure every day and I am blessed to call Fred FRIEND."

I remember some rough trips with Hatfield as well. We used to room together on the road, and once Hatfield got bit by a dog while he was jogging around a Holiday Inn by the airport in Miami. Another time after the AFA liason officer in Miami made a big deal about the head coach of the AFA coming to visit. Ken got in the rental car without realizing that he had stepped in dog poop. Needless to say, he didn't make the great impression that the officer was expecting. We were used to recruiting in December because we weren't good enough to go to bowl games yet. When Ken sent us out on the road, we were out for three weeks at a time. After the first three years, we started seeing other coaches going home and asked Ken why we had to be sitting in hotel rooms on the weekends. Ken just said no one ever told us we couldn't go home. Later we found out the AFA had an unlimited budget for recruiting.

I continued looking for talent and brains over brawn, just as we had done at Florida A&M. I took players sledding and even took Ted Sundquist, who wanted to be a vet, out to the stables to see my daughter's horse. I figured if Ted loved animals, he might want to be around them. It didn't matter that the Academy didn't have a vet program. I convinced Ted to change his major and come anyway.

Fisher DeBerry says, "Fred was a great recruiter. He had a lot to do with me coming to the Academy. He called every night and made me think I was going to hell if I didn't come to the AFA. He made it sound like the next best place to heaven on earth."

The first year was rough. In 1979, our record was 2-9 and 26 true freshmen played. We lost badly against Notre Dame, 59-33, but gained experience playing a Fighting Irish team that would go on to the Sugar Bowl. We implemented the flexbone in spring practice. In the first game, against Tulsa, I was coaching special teams and was unable to defend against future Chicago Bear Lovey Smith. It crushed me when Ken told me that special teams cost us the game. I almost got in trouble again when I missed the opening kickoff of the Georgia Tech game because I was up in the press box eating a barbeque sandwich and talking to Jerri Spurrier. We would go on to lose the first eight games of the season. There was not much pressure to win and expectations were low. We were everyone's homecoming game. Finally we beat Army, but Pam put that victory in perspective, saying, "It looked like two teams going in slow motion." The most encouraging game was a win over Vandy on Nov.17, 1979. Andy Bark caught a Hail Mary touchdown pass from Dave Ziebart with no time left on the clock. According to retired Gen. O, Sampson, "That would catapult AFA teams from that point on to greater success and put Air Force on the map with other prominent football programs."

Fisher DeBerry was the key to turning the offense around. After a year at the Academy, Hatfield had decided to put in the triple option that DeBerry had been using at Appalachian State. In 1980, Fisher DeBerry became the quarterback coach and implemented the wishbone. Twenty freshmen played. Shawn Smith said:

> None of us was ever going to go pro. We played because we wanted to, and it was an opportunity to play Division I football. We played for the love of the game. We played for the team, and not for self.

It took awhile to get used to the wishbone even though quarterback Marty Louthan could run it well. We had to move good offensive guys to defense to improve speed. Since we were smaller, we had to rely on speed, brains, and good technique. Because of the structured environment and tight schedule at the Academy, the coaches knew we had a limited amount of time to work on the game plan.

We installed a simple "bend not break" defense to make opponents go the long, hard way and wear them out so they would make mistakes and our offense would get the ball back. The players were still having trouble with fundamentals and fumbling the ball on exchanges. We were overmatched physically but knew what the defense could look like with better players. We also brought in Jack Braley, a new strength coach. The AFA ended the season 2-9-1 but we learned how to defend the wishbone during practice and beat our first WAC opponent, Pat Dye's 9-1 Wyoming squad. Our other victory came against a bowl bound Navy team.

The Falcons played hard and kept the score surprisingly close with a 24-10 loss in the 1980 Notre Dame game. The Irish head coach, Dan Devine, wouldn't stop throwing the ball, even when they had it won with a couple minutes to go. They could have run the ball and killed the clock, and the game would have been over. Chan Gailey was up in the press box talking to me over the radio, "They're trying to run the score up. Tell Ken not to let them get away with it." Ken wouldn't say anything. Chan yelled, "You just go tell him off, Fred!" I said, "You're right Chan!" I didn't realize the radio guy was standing beside Dan when I said some choice words. Ken had walked off without shaking his hand, so when I stormed across the field the Notre Dame people thought I was Hatfield. I wondered why the priest was so nice to me when he let me into the locker room to apologize. They never knew it was me.

Pam was watching the sports with her parents and saw it on the news that night. It got out in the paper the next day and eventually died down. When the team played in Hawaii Pam was still upset, so all the other coaches thought it was funny to bring it back

up and try to get me in trouble. They never realized
just how hurt and embarrassed she was. That happened
around Thanksgiving, and the convention was usually
in early January. The coaches had been out recruiting
and it had died down pretty well. When I went to pick
up Ken at the airport, he had been reading an article
about Devine on the plane. John Makovich was
teasing him on the plane thinking Ken was the one
who had lost his temper. Even Hatfield's own mother,
Billie Lou, didn't know the truth for awhile. When she
found out about it, she told Ken, "Good for Fred!" She
was glad someone finally told off Dan Devine.
Hatfield said, "It took eight months to convince Dan
Devine and a national magazine that it was Fred and
not me that had talked to coach Divine."

When I was 37, just before the 1981 season, I
was offered the head coaching job at Slippery Rock
State College by President Herb Reinhardt, a former
vice president at FAMU. His son was our kicker, and
is now the athletic director at Valdosta State. Their
coach had retired in July, so I was hired late and kept
the old staff. The players couldn't get comfortable with
the new offense and defense, and our quarterback
broke his ankle in the first game and was out for the
season. Slippery Rock played Wayne State in Ann
Arbor, Michigan in the first game. We went for two at
the end of the game and lost 14-13, even though the
game film showed we had gotten the two-point
conversion. They didn't have instant replay back then,
and the ruling stood. A highlight of that season was
upsetting Edinboro on ESPN when our All American,

Rick Porter, had a sensational game. I forgot to tell Pam that I had invited all the coaches and their families over to watch the ESPN replay of the game and have breakfast the next morning, so we had to run out late at night and buy groceries. It was a tough season going 2-7, and those seven games we lost were by a total of 26 points. Nothing about that move went smoothly. When I had the opportunity to go back to the Academy as linebacker coach and assistant head coach, I was ready to go. We were stuck with a house in Pennsylvania for seven years. When we thought we had finally found a buyer in 1987, the stock market crashed and the man couldn't buy our house because he was a stockbroker and lost his money.

When I got back to the AFA, Chan Gailey had been promoted to defensive coordinator. Gailey said:

When he came back six months later, and I was the defensive coordinator he never made me feel threatened or inadequate even though I know he knew more than me. He would listen to decisions from a young coach and never make me feel dumb. He handled that so professionally, and I have tried to emulate his actions when I have gone from being a head coach back to an assistant.

The Falcons had improved in 1981. AFA player Jeff Hays says:

> The AFA had not won in a decade, and I credit Coach Hatfield and John Clune for putting them in the Western Athletic Conference and hiring Fisher DeBerry to run the offense. We

didn't look like a college team until 1981. The athletes were used to losing and it took a certain mentality to take a losing team and win 18 games in two years. We had 26 freshmen on our travel squad.

In 1982, I returned to a team that had gone 4-7 the year before and beaten a PAC 10 Oregon team. We were more confident and starting to feel like we could whip anyone. It would be a year of firsts for Falcon football; it would be the first time we would beat Notre Dame, bring home the Commander in Chief trophy, and win a bowl game. The Falcons beat BYU and their all-pro quarterback Steve Young by driving 99 yards in 90 seconds with no time outs and getting the two point conversion to win 39-38. We also beat Army and Navy to win the Commander in Chief Trophy. But, the biggest win was the 30-17 win over Notre Dame for the first time in school history. One of the best plays in that game was an exciting quarterback sneak and 65 yard run to the one yard line. Center Ricard Smith and quarterback Marty Louthan had seen a hole and called their own play. The headline on the sports page that Sunday read the name of a popular song, "O What a Feeling", and the subtitle was "The Falcon Bone Chokes the Irish". With eight wins, the AFA was eligible for a bowl. When Cal had their miracle win over Stanford by running a kickoff return through the Stanford band and scoring, they put the Falcons in the Hall of Fame bowl against Vanderbilt on New Year's Eve. Hatfield recalled:

Due to the heavy snow and rain, we only got to practice two days. Fred was livid. He said he needed more practice time to stop them. I told him we couldn't stop them with 30 days of practice so concentrate on getting turnovers. Vanderbilt passed like crazy with one player catching 21 passes (still a standing bowl record), but our defense came up with five turnovers and stopped them one inch short on the last play to preserve a 36-28 victory. It was Air Force's first bowl victory ever.

"A select group of coaches helped bright, undersized young men to achieve what nobody else thought possible. It was thrilling to watch this unfold!" said Gen. O. Sampson. Safety Chuck Petersen added, "That staff took kids to a higher level than anyone ever dreamed they could go and influenced their lives way beyond football."

In 1983, the Falcons won the Commander and Chief trophy again and improved their record to 10-2, rising to 13th in the nation in the AP polls. The biggest victory was another miracle win over Notre Dame. A small AFA defense had to stop Steve Beuerlein and Allen Pinkett. Beuerlein played 17 years in the NFL and Pinkett was an All American and Heisman contender who rushed for over 1100 yards each season and still holds the Notre Dame record for career scoring with 53 touchdowns. The smallest Notre Dame players were 6'5" 275 lbs., while AFA safety Greg Zollinger was 5'10" 170 lbs. Zollinger tried to stop 6'4" 250lb. All American, All Pro tight end Mark

Bavarro. It was a close game with the score going back and forth. On the final drive, Notre Dame drove 50 yards to the 10 with a few minutes left. Our coaches thought we had lost the game and called a timeout while the Irish were setting up to kick a field goal. John Carney, the Notre Dame kicker, was so strong that he played in the NFL until 2009. He was the oldest player at age 45 and became the third leading career scorer in the NFL with 2,044 points. Fisher prayed and said, "Fred, don't worry about it, we're prepared, and we're going to block that kick." I knew we couldn't get through the line, so we couldn't block the kick unless they all jumped. Chris Funk got the block. Chris didn't have the academic record the other recruits had coming into the Academy. He was there on a presidential scholarship because his dad had served three tours of duty in Vietnam. But, he thought like the coaches and could understand what we wanted. The others rushed forward, but Funk was the one who listened and jumped. There was stunned silence in the Notre Dame stadium. The silence was broken as we were walking up the tunnel and a Notre Dame fan said, "Damn, our wives are bigger than these guys."

Hatfield said:

The victories over Notre Dame in 1982 and 1983 were such team affairs, but our small but gutsy defenders came up with big stops many, many times in critical situations to come up with 31-17 and 23-21 wins.

The Falcons went on to beat Ole Miss 9-3 in the Independence Bowl in Shreveport, LA. We thought we might go to the Liberty Bowl, but the bowl director of the Liberty Bowl was a Notre Dame graduate. He told Ken Hatfield the week before the game that they would take Notre Dame win or lose because the Irish were having a down year and the Liberty Bowl might not have a chance to get them again. It made Ken mad and he said, "Mr. Dudley, next Saturday we're gonna embarass you, your school, and your bowl. We're gonna whip their butts on Saturday." Right before that phone call, Ken had called me into his office and told me how much Notre Dame had improved and said he didn't think we could cover Mark Bavarro. He didn't think we had a chance to win. That season set the tempo for the next three years and made our teams believe they could find a way to win.

Sundquist, a player and coach at the Academy, added:

> They created a positive environment. That influence not only affected the teams Hatfield coached, but the players I recruited are now colonels and generals. They affected the leadership of the Academy and the Air Force in general. Players were encouraged to stick it out. Football was important but we knew our coaches thought our futures were just as important."

Woo Pig Sooie

In 1984, Hatfield took the Arkansas job and brought most of his assistants with him. Fisher DeBerry remained as the Falcon head coach for the next 23 years, becoming the most successful head coach in AFA history. Ken Hatfield had played on the 1964 National Championship team at Arkansas so that was probably the only job that could have lured him away from the Academy. He told his staff that the whole state was behind the football program, and he was right. Large crowds of fans would bring their RVs to watch spring practice and camp out in the parking lot of Broyles Stadium. When the coaches went out to recruit, they were introduced as coaches from The University. Restaurants had Razorback wallpaper and door mats and even the sugar packets had Razorbacks on them. Quarterback Greg Thomas said:

> Hearing the fans call the Hogs was the strangest thing I'd ever seen grown people do. I liked walking through the fans with a police escort. It's hard to explain what it feels like to have everyone in the stadium calling the Hogs.

I agree. There is nothing like riding the bus from Conway to Little Rock on game day and seeing thousands of fans cheering for the team.

There were many wonderful boosters, but one that made a lasting impression on me was Willeen McKinnon. She was 90 years old when she started writing Ken and me letters of encouragement. She became like a grandmother to us, and I would write to her until her death at age 98. I called her on Dec.23, 1996 and the last thing she said to me was, 'I love you, Fred.' She died later that night.

In the first recruiting meeting, I had the impression that I would do most of my recruiting in Arkansas and Texas, so I was a little surprised when Hatfield told me to go to Stuttgart. I was used to having some international recruits at the USAFA and thought he meant Stuttgart, Germany instead of Stuttgart, Arkansas. Because of the intensely loyal alumni and a SWC Cotton Bowl tradition, we could keep most of the Arkansas talent in state. The players have a saying, "Once a Razorback, always a Razorback", and many sons grow up wanting to play for the Hogs.

Since we had been recruiting Texas, I went back to Stratford High School in Houston on my first recruiting trip for Arkansas. We had been interested in a recruit for the AFA, and thought we could persuade him to go to the U of A. The mother had wanted him to go to the Academy, and she took me outside and told me in no uncertain terms, "I'm going to tell you something. I'll pay my boy's way to any other school before I'll let him go to Ole Miss or Arkansas."

Sometimes, the new recruits took awhile to adjust to college ball. Matt Pitner and Kenny Kearnes were both from Memorial High School in Houston. One bad practice when Kenny was fumbling the exchange, Hatfield said, "What's wrong with you two? You played together in high school." Pittman responded, "He couldn't get my snaps in high school either."

In 1984, Hatfield had to clean up a program that lacked discipline and had one of the worst graduation rates in the country. Players who had been there under the old regime said it was a wild group of kids. They were some pretty rough city kids. Once, Steve Atwater's girlfriend's ex-boyfriend showed up at the dorm with a gun. Ma Kettle, the dorm mom, called me. I said Bobby Trott and I would be right over. I don't know what I thought we'd do when we got there. I'm just glad he was gone by then. They used to rig up their beds to look like they were there at bed check and sneak off campus to party. Hatfield whipped them into shape by making them run stairs and study and suspending them when they got out of line. Most of the players that were there in 1984 saw positive changes and were relieved to have some order instituted.

U of A assistant coach Tim Horton also remembers our notorious work ethic. He said, "As a player, I never went into a game unprepared. He was so detailed and thorough. I try to do some of the same things today." Chuck Petersen was a graduate assistant at Arkansas during that year and remembers learning how to develop the work ethic required in a good coach. He recalls:

> Coach Goldsmith's preparation was amazing... we had already been invited to the Liberty Bowl... our opponent was yet to be determined. Coach was convinced we were going to play LSU and had me break down the 10 games they had already played. He put together a game plan based on that information. Unfortunately for me, we ended up playing Auburn and I had to break down the 11 games they played so he could develop a game plan for them. What that experience taught me as a young coach is that there is detail in the preparation and that every detail is important.

The reason I was so sure we were going to play LSU was because all Auburn had to do to go to the Sugar Bowl was to beat Alabama, and Lewis Campbell the secondary coach at Alabama had assured Bobby Trott that they could not defeat Auburn. Alabama pulled a big upset in the last minute of the game when Bo Jackson collided with another Auburn back, and Alabama stopped them on the goal line. Consequently, I gave my LSU breakdown to a Nebraska coach who would be playing them in the Sugar Bowl.

Ironically, my daughter was reading an article in a preseason magazine projecting Bo Jackson as a Heisman contender. She said, "Dad this guy is good, I'm glad we don't have to play him this year."

I said, "Don't worry about that, we won't have to play him." Then we ended up losing to Auburn and Bo Jackson in the Liberty Bowl. It was a building year and the Razorbacks went 7-4-1.

Not only did we want to be prepared as coaches, but we expected the players to be prepared, so we were tough on them in practice. Even though we had an indoor practice field, the coaches liked to practice outside in the rain to be prepared for game day conditions. None of the players wanted to be out there. Steve Atwater said, "He would dive on the ball as if recovering a fumble, and the defense all thought he was crazy, but it ended any problems we had practicing or playing in the rain. If Coach could do it, so could we." Secondary coach Bobby Trott said he remembers us staying out there even when there was golf ball sized hail. I would say, "It's not that bad. Where's Otis, make sure we haven't lost him with this water level." Otis was about 5'6".

Steven Jones, current President of the Dallas Cowboys, was moved from quarterback to defense during the coaching transition. He describes me as "very intense, and that's probably an understatement". His first start was at the Orange Bowl, and the Razorbacks were getting ready for it by practicing in Fayetteville in freezing rain and ice. There was about a

30 mile an hour wind. The defense was pouting because the offense got to be inside using the indoor facility No one had much intensity. Jones explained:

> When you are real cold you move around a little timid. To get them fired up, Goldsmith started screaming, 'What is it with you guys. Are you worried about this stuff?' He took a running start from about 15 yards and slid like Superman. There was ice in his hair and even in his eyebrows and he said 'This stuff won't hurt you men!' The players said, 'If he can jump in the middle of this ice, we can too' and we went on and had a good practice.

According to Eric Bradford, I started screaming that it wasn't cold and then ran and dove on the ground like a kid playing on a slip and slide. "We were shocked beyond belief that he would just jump on the ground and get soaking wet. But it worked. After he did that, we started executing better."

Kerry Crawford remembered a similar incident on another cold, icy day. They were running a drill and a running back dropped the ball. The ball hit the ground and all the players just stood there looking at the ball on the ground. They weren't about to touch the ball. Kerry says:

> Coach Goldsmith wanted us to be mentally alert and never, ever let the ball hit the ground. He came unglued when he saw us all standing around and screamed so loud we could see the veins sticking out on his neck. We thought he

was gonna have a heart attack or something. He dove on the ground grabbed the ball, rolled around and picked the ball up, jumped on me, jumped off me, still screaming. It was the funniest thing I've ever seen. The poor players were scared half to death. We thought we were all gonna die if we didn't get that ball. He was a very intense coach.

Orthopaedic surgeon and former player Owen Kelly remembers me installing a love for the game and for the players. They couldn't slack off in practice. Owen said, "If you were covering the pass rush, he would say, 'Do not jump.' One time we saw him throw his hat on the ground and get mad at a player. He said, 'You didn't jump but you were thinking about it!'"

The 1985 season got off to a rocky start. The players and fans didn't like the offense at first and some of the Arkansas fans had a problem with quarterback Greg Thomas because he was black. Martin Lemont had been the first black quarterback eight years before, but he only lasted one semester because of the pressure. One painful memory I have is of the Ole Miss game. Greg Thomas endured racial slurs from the crowd of 53,000 when we played in Jackson. I thought Ole Miss was booing him at first but he said, "Coach, those are our fans." Later Thomas said:

I wanted to prove I could play there. It was unbelievably hard pressure. It is hard enough just being a Razorback quarterback because it is so different than any other institution because deep down the football program represents the entire state. You're the hero or the goat. Coach Goldsmith told me that a million times.

If it wasn't for Coach Goldsmith, I wouldn't have gotten a chance to play at all. He let me run the scout team and told the quarterback coach, David Lee, to give me a chance to play quarterback. We had a great relationship. He went out of his way to make sure I was always comfortable and was always encouraging. Even if I played bad, he was one of the first coaches to walk over and pat me on the back and tell me not to worry about it. He went out of the way to do things with and for me.

Thomas remembers me putting on my own halftime show one week:

He was one of the most intense coaches I've ever seen in my life. I remember one game we were playing poorly. At halftime, he walked right past me so fired up you could almost see the whites of his eyes. He had beads of sweat on his forehead and kicked over the table, sending Gatorade and oranges flying. He went on a rampage about 30 seconds, then he stopped and said, 'Alright, that half is over, now everyone come out like Fighting Razorbacks, go to your coach and we'll get this thing corrected.' I thought this man had done lost his mind. It scared the snot out of me for a little bit and then I went on and did what I had to do, he confronted the defensive players, and we went out and won the game pretty handily.

The 1985 defense went through the whole SWC, a running conference, without allowing a rushing touchdown. Player Limbo Parks said, "It was freaking awesome. As the defensive line coach at Lee's Summit West High School, I have adopted his philosophy that nobody runs the football against us."

The U of A played a great Baylor team in 1985. Linebacker Nick Miller intercepted a pass in the end zone right before the half to stop their drive. In the second half, All-Conference noseguard Tony Cherico called Baylor's snap count, causing them to jump off sides twice. I didn't tell him to do it, but Hatfield said, "If he ever does it again, I'll fire you." Now, a defensive line coach in Northwest Arkansas, Cherico remembers me looking out for him:

> He genuinely cared for us. He would come by and check on us. I was suspended for the TCU game and he came by and gave us a pep talk. I couldn't ask for a better coach to emulate, not just with the Xs and 0s but how to treat people.

We didn't have a lot to work with defensively in those early years at Arkansas. We were the smallest in the conference but our staff had experience working with undersized players. The ability to run was always the priority over size. Kevin Anderson remembers my philosophy, "It didn't matter how much bigger or faster any team was than us, if we hit them hard enough, we could always bring them down to our size and win. It works. I use his phrases and ideas when coaching a 9-10 year old Razorback team." Even two time Super Bowl champion Steve Atwater had a learning curve that first year. "Due to a touchdown caused by us not all swarming to the ball, I learned the importance of not stopping until the whistle blows," Steve said. Rick Apolskis mentioned another fundamental saying of ours, "You can kill a mosquito with an ax." That meant don't ease up on a bad team; play hard every play.

Sometimes, the coaches learned from the players. Rodney Beachum got tired of being fussed at for not lifting weights. He was about 230 lbs. and one of the best players on the team. He finally said, "I can bench 300 lbs. Nobody we play weighs over 300 lbs., so as long as I can move them out of the way, what's the problem?" It made sense to me, and I never bothered him about it again.

Hatfield's 1985 team was loaded with talent. We would go 50 straight quarters without allowing any rushing touchdowns. We lost a close 10-6 game against Texas A&M and turned the ball over four times in a heartbreaking 15-13 loss to Texas. At the end of the season, the U of A would be ranked number 12 in the nation with a 10-2 record. Typical of the defense that year, we would make another impressive goal line stand to defeat Arizona State in the Holiday Bowl.

In 1986, the Holtz recruits graduated and Cherico joked with me, "Now all these good players have graduated, you're gonna have to do some coaching." The Razorbacks maintained our momentum with a 9-3 record. The Texas A&M game was the sweetest victory. The Aggies were the best team in the conference, and their quarterback, Kevin Murray, had broken his ankle the previous year and wasn't running the ball much. We had seen their film and noticed that one of their big tackles would give away whether it was a run or pass by his foot position. Our scout team had practiced imitating this guy, and we were able to flush the quarterback out of the pocket and pull off a big upset. The next day we got a bowl bid to the Orange Bowl. We lost to Oklahoma in the Orange Bowl, but finished the season number 15 in the AP poll.

Despite a 9-4 record, and an impressive 1,000 yard rushing record set by James Rouse, and the fact that we led the conference in rushing and scoring defense, Hatfield and I came under fire after losing to Texas on the last play of the game in 1987. Greg Thomas separated his shoulder during the game, and I got hit from behind by a receiver and blew my knee out. Time out was called before the last play, and there was a good plan in place, but a linebacker was out of position. Despite Steve Atwater blasting him, the Texas receiver made an unbelievable catch behind his back, pinned the ball to his hip, and fell into the end zone. Even though everyone had chances to make plays throughout the game, I blamed myself for the coverage and for the ensuing tension between Hatfield and Broyles. Broyles pressured Hatfield to fire me after the game, but Hatfield refused. We went on to lose to Georgia in the Liberty Bowl. With a minute to go the score was tied 17-17. The defense made a great stop in what we thought would be Georgia's last possession. On the first play after that, we threw a pass interception to give them great field position. They kicked a field goal on the last play of the game to win.

1988 was the year that Arkansas led the nation in turnover margin, was fourth in rushing defense, and had four all SWC performers. The highlight of the year was beating Texas A&M in the last game in Fayetteville. Patrick Williams scored a defensive touchdown and we won the game by a score of 25-20 to secure the conference championship. Kerry Owens tackled A&M for a safety, giving the Hogs two more points. Ken Hatfield said:

> At Arkansas, the key was a great defense and Fred always prepared one. We went 10-0 before losing to a great Miami team 18-16. The 1988 Fighting Razorbacks had eight guys that started for three years as they drove the bus to the first SWC Championship in 13 years.

The chant heard around campus for weeks was, "Hey Hey Ho Ho Arkansas to the Cotton Bowl". Arkansas would play Troy Aikman and UCLA in the Cotton Bowl, and would remain number 12 in the AP Poll. Kendall Trainer would kick his twenty-fourth field goal in a row to keep the game from being a shutout as Arkansas lost 17-3.

According to quarterback Greg Thomas, the Hatfield years were the best five years in Arkansas Razorback history, and the ability Hatfield's teams had to unify the state has gone unparalleled. Those teams were tight, and Thomas still stays in touch with 85% of his graduating class. Many of Hatfield's players were drafted by the pros including: Steve Atwater, an eight time Pro Bowler and two time Super Bowl champion with the Denver Broncos, Ravin Caldwell, a two time Super Bowl Champion with the Washington Redskins, Barry Foster, a Pro Bowler who set a single season rushing record of 1,690 yards for the Pittsburgh Steelers, Kevin Anderson, Rick Apolskis, Richard Brothers, Freddie Childress, Greg Lasker, Jim Mabry, Wayne Martin, Nick Miller, James Rouse, Kevin Wyatt and Theo Young.

The players knew we cared about them even when they messed up. Manager John Petersen told this story:

> I will never, ever forget this. We were playing Texas A&M in College Station on national television. During the games it was my job to hold the cord for Coach Goldsmith's headset. This was before wireless technology. The cords were very long and Coach had a way of moving frequently during a game. Well, this game is on national TV and during one of the TV timeouts Coach is running up the sideline to the huddle. In my haste to keep up, I didn't realize that the cord had gotten tangled with the yard markers, so when we broke from the timeout,

his cord was all wrapped up. It was really wrapped up pretty bad, and we could not get it untangled. The ref starts yelling and saying this will cost us a timeout if we can't get it untangled. Everyone is scrambling to help and it seems like it's taking forever. Coach Hatfield starts screaming, which was fairly uncharacteristic of him. The really funny thing is… Coach Goldsmith never got upset. Once we got it untangled, he just gave me the biggest smile. Years later, Coach Goldsmith and Mrs. Goldsmith came to my wedding, and it meant more to me than if President George Bush had walked in.

Linebacker Ty Mason said, "There was a rare and special bond on that staff. I was blessed to have the opportunity to play for them and go to church with some of the staff. I remember Coach Goldsmith used to draw up plays on the bulletins." Greg Thomas reiterated:

I am a better person, coach, Christian, and father through all those experiences playing for Arkansas and some real good mentors. The examples were always present. Everything I do goes back to that, including my relationships at home and with coaches, and what I will and will not allow with my players now.

Just as we had done with Derek Foster at the USAFA, the coaches prayed for injured players. Kevin Anderson remembers Coach Hatfield, his wife Sandy, and me praying and telling him that God had moved mountains and He would get him through a dislocated shoulder injury. The doctors decided not to perform surgery and instead of missing the season, Kevin only missed three games, his shoulder healed, and he was able to play in the Holiday Bowl.

Linebacker Nick Miller knew I cared about his spiritual condition as well:

> Coach Goldsmith led me to the Lord my senior year. It meant a lot to me that he cared that much. I had always believed in God, just had not plugged in, and was not living my life like I knew I should. He forced me to face how I was living, and I have never been the same since.

Many players look up to their coaches as father figures, and for Kerry Crawford, whose single mom raised a family of 17 brothers and sisters, I was honored to play that role:

> I've always appreciated him for being a man of his word and teaching us to stand up and be strong. He taught us to be men; he was a great motivator, he told great stories, and he didn't back down from a challenge. He was always on top of things and a no nonsense kind of guy. I loved him because he was genuine. He always told me the truth.

A good coach is honest with his players and will own up to his mistakes. Crawford recalls that he had only played football one year in high school and

his terminology was limited. When he arrived at
Arkansas, I was looking to play him at linebacker and
told him to stand on the hash. Crawford didn't even
know what a hash was, so I thought he wouldn't be
able to handle the linebacker position. In his junior
year, I called Kerry into my office and told him I had
misjudged him. I didn't think he was smart enough to
play linebacker, but he was one of our best students
and did an excellent job for us. Crawford remembers:

> I never understood why he took me out of the
> linebacking core. I thought I was out there to
> learn the position; he presumed I couldn't cut it
> mentally, and when he told me years later, then
> I understood. It helped me know that unless
> you make people know where you are coming
> from, they won't know how to appreciate you.

Why Not Rice?

During the Cotton Bowl Ball, Gil Brandt, the Vice President of the Cowboys and Fred Jacoby, Commissioner of the Southwest Conference, told me Jerry Berndt had resigned at Rice and asked if I would be interested in the job. Assistants get to be head coaches in three situations. Either the head coach is fired, quits in disgust, or retires from a successful program. The last one is a golden opportunity. Unfortunately, my situation was the first one. They had been winless the year before and Jerry Berndt's contract was not renewed. When I told my daughter I was interested in the job, she said, "Why Rice?" It was hard for her to understand why I would leave Arkansas to take a chance on a school that had a reputation for losing. Jerry Moore was standing next to me when the question was posed. He was on our Arkansas staff and knew John Cox from his days at Texas Tech. Cox was a Midland, TX oil man on Rice's Board of Trustees. Moore called for me and Gil Brandt (who had also helped Mr. Cox get Watson Brown, Mack Brown's brother, a job as the Rice head coach) called and recommended me. Bucky Allshouse from the Rice

Board called me and made the arrangements for our visit.

I flew to Houston on Sunday and interviewed at River Oaks Country Club with Evans Atwell, Chairman of the Board, and Charles Duncan, president of Coca Cola Foods. I was overwhelmed by the country club, especially when someone said, "Son this is where we make presidents." Bobby May was the assistant AD at the time, and when I asked if he would be the AD, he said, "Well, if we can hire someone like you, I will be, but if they try to get a big name, we'll probably have to give him the AD job too and I'll still be sitting here as an assistant. They were big on the honor code at Rice, and they liked that I could still recite the USAFA honor code, "We don't lie, cheat or steal or tolerate those who do". They also called Joe Paterno, and I am sure it helped to have a good reference from him.

When I got the job, I had been recruiting in Houston since 1979 and knew I had to hire coaches from Texas or those who had familiarity with recruiting there. Craig Bohl had recruited Houston and I knew him because he had come to the U of A to visit and talk defense when he was an assistant coach at Tulsa. Bohl said that when he told his mom about the new job she wanted to plan her vacations around bowl games. He told her we were ranked ninth out of nine teams in the SWC and not to worry about any bowl games. He told me later that he wondered if he was committing professional suicide by agreeing to come to Rice. Mike Heimerdinger had been with me at Air

Force. Bohl and Dinger were coordinators with me at Rice and Duke. Dinger would later end up with two Super Bowl rings while at the Denver Broncos. Both Bohl and Dinger were good coordinators. Next we got Dean Campbell, who had coached at Texas, Texas A&M and UNC. He brought in a lot of key players from San Antonio. He knew how to recruit the SWC; he was well connected to Texas high school coaches. Later he left for Texas Tech, and we replaced him with Hardy McCrary. Hardy did a wonderful job with our secondary and fit right in. I also tried to get J.B. Grimes. His brother Carl was one of my best friends from Fayetteville, but we lost a bidding war with Mississippi State over him. Next I hired Mike Bender from South Carolina; he had been a teammate of Hatfield's at the U of A. Scotty Conley had coached at UT and Tennessee, and Keith Burns, a product of L.D. Bell High school in Dallas, had been a graduate assistant at Arkansas and was a coordinator at Pacific. He could coach the secondary or receivers. Wayne Hooks and Dave Cope were also Texas high school coaches. Dinger knew a guy named Steve Carson on the West Coast, and we hired him part-time to help with the receivers. He became a valuable part of our staff. Later I hired Pete Hurt, Bryant Poole, David Moody, Les Koenning Jr. Jeff McInerney and Joe DeForest, and I hired John Zernheldt to replace Mike Bender after he went to UNLV. John did a super job as our offensive line coach helping Trevor Cobb to break SWC rushing records.

The first time I met with the team, they knew nobody wanted the job, but they were so glad to have a coach that they gave me a standing ovation. Max Moss told me that he was so happy to have a Christian coach that he didn't care if I knew anything about football. The players' support was important at that time because I had been stuck in horrible Houston traffic the night before questioning why I ever left Fayetteville, AR. Moving from a small town back to a big city was a big adjustment for both Pam and I. It had been years since we had lived in Miami. Pam is reserved by nature, but she has learned to be flexible during all our moves and adapted well to the role of a head coach's wife. Right after I was hired, a Rice fundraiser auctioned off a dinner with the Rice football coach. Someone bid hundreds of dollars to eat with Pam and me. We hadn't even unpacked yet, so we had to serve them on Wal-Mart china. Pam was mortified when the president of Shell Oil showed up for dinner.

I wasn't hired until Jan.16, a couple of weeks before signing date. Jimmy Golden was the only commitment Rice had on the books when we started. Trevor Cobb, our first commitment, would become an All American and win the Doak Walker award. He was the greatest back in Rice history. Alonzo Williams, a four year starter, also played a key role in helping us win. Alonzo was active in FCA and spoke to churches in the Houston community with me. Greg Willig was our backup quarterback and starting quarterback after Donald Hollas graduated. Later Willig was a GA for me at Duke.

The players were excited about playing for us. Williams told David Bachert of The Houston Post, "He's a players' coach. It's hard to find a coach who is concerned about his players. The guys see he's really genuine and want to play for him."

Matt Sign from Arlington, Lamar was one of the most promising recruits. At 5'10" 210 lbs., he was too little for Arkansas, but I liked him because he was similar to Cherico. In my office, Matt's dad swore Matt was 225 lbs., and then Matt ran in after weighing in and yelled, "I finally got to 210!" He came in with a big pair of boots on to make him look taller. Sign beat out everyone to become the all time tackler for losses in Rice history and was All Conference for three years. Matt was a tremendous player. Matt's brothers were highly recruited by Pitt and Alabama, but Matt turned out to be the best.

We didn't have a sponsor for the first TV show, so Matt's Dad, Bob, got Seagrams to sponsor us for Canada Dry. The commercials didn't arrive on time for the first show, and we had to ad lib some Canada Dry commercials during the show.

Chris Miller, a transfer from Fayetteville, Arkansas, was also a great holder for extra points and field goals. Of course there were some difficulties to overcome. Rice hadn't had a winning record in nearly 30 years. The players had never seen Rice win in their lifetimes. When I gave a recruiting report at the first quarterback club meeting, some fella with red hair stood up and told me, "We haven't won in years and you aren't gonna win here either." I saw him at the 2012 Rice spring game and he came up and apologized. He told me he had become a Christian and that he wasn't the same person now that he was then. We would also have to change the Rice mindset of excellence in academics but not athletics. Rice wasn't successful in any sports at a time when they were competing with schools like Texas and Texas A&M that excelled in both sports and academics. I told them it was great to play well and not win, but that's not what we were here for. We expected to win when we stepped out on the field.

Our philosophy was, "Don't ever look back and say we were afraid to try to win. If you win, you win, if you don't you don't. But don't ever be prepared not to win a game." I would always say, "Hay is never in the barn." That meant we could never be prepared enough for a game.

We started with Keith Burns on receivers, but noticed in spring practice that year that we were dull on defense personality wise. There wasn't that guy with the rah rah to make us upbeat. Ken had taught me that you can never change people's personalities. Instead, use their personalities to make the staff the way you want it to be. I am glad Ken shared that with me. He knew it wouldn't hurt for him to give me advice because he didn't consider us a threat in the SWC. The U of A was battling A&M and Texas for the conference championship, and we were just trying to break a losing streak. I asked Dinger to work with the quarterbacks and hired Joe DeForest to work with the running backs. We organized the position coaches according to where the personalities fit.

In March, I had back surgery and missed the first spring game. When I was getting my MRI before the surgery, Dicky Maegle called me in the hospital and told me to hightail it out of there because he had had the same procedure and it was too painful. It was too late because I was already on the gurney. Dicky Maegle was a Rice All American who gained 265 yards in the Cotton Bowl when Rice beat Alabama. That was a strange game. Maegle was awarded a touchdown because an Alabama linebacker had come off the bench and tackled him.

One of the players Rice had worked hard to get was Voddie Bauchum. Voddie transferred in from New Mexico to Rice and could play linebacker or tight end; he was a good looking athlete who could do everything well. Rice had some strong Christian kids that went to a FCA retreat in Austin one weekend and Voddie went with them. Monday morning Voddie came in all excited to see me because he had become a Christian. Then he went on and had a good week of practice. The next Monday he came in with his head down and said he was leaving Rice. He said he had gone to church and gotten ordained on Sunday, and that he had to leave to be a preacher. So there goes my best player off to Houston Baptist, a school that didn't even have a football team. Today he is one of the great evangelists and authors; he did everything he said he would and went on to seminary and got his PhD.

Several of the Owls went into the pros. Larry Izzo became a Pro Bowler at Miami, Donald Hollas, O.J. Brigance, Bert Emmanuel, Greg King, Richard Segina, and Jimmy Lee all went pro. Kurt Roper is now the offensive coordinator at Duke. Kurt always tells a story about Rice training camp and teases me about it to this day. I was getting fed up with the players throwing their banana peels on the ground when nobody was looking, and told them, "A guy who throws banana peels on the floor when he thinks nobody is looking will cheat on his wife when nobody's looking." That story has gotten exaggerated over the years. When I saw Shane Hollas recently, he said he remembers me always harping on them about eating breakfast. He told me I said, "If you miss breakfast, you'll cheat on your wife one day." Shane said he never missed breakfast and is happily married. I was referring to the biblical principle that if they weren't faithful in the little things like picking up after themselves, they wouldn't be faithful in the big things. Hollas said:

> You did an excellent job of strengthening my belief in God. I don't know how many college coaches out there today are as outwardly demonstrative as you were, but I cannot help but think that there aren't near as many as inspiring.

The Rice players were smart and had character. They were at a disadvantage because of the strenuous academic requirements, and they were smaller than the other players in the conference, but they were focused, hard workers just like the cadets at the Air Force Academy. They responded well when we had to make decisions that put the team ahead of their individual goals. Hollas remembers a meeting we had:

> Another thing about you that reminded me of my father was how honest you were. When you had to sit Tim Winn and me down to inform us that a freshman, Kolis Crier, was going to start in place of both of us, I almost felt betrayed. However, after a period of time, I came to realize and respect that you were doing what was necessary and that Kolis was indeed a better choice. The fact that you brought us in and told us face to face was very admirable.

Pam and I enjoyed Houston. Her sister and brother-in-law, Penny and Bill Ross lived there. We got involved in Sugar Creek Baptist Church. Our pastor, Fenton Morehead, got the church involved with Pam's benevolence ministry that she had started in Colorado Springs and continued at University Baptist Church in Fayetteville, AR under H.D. McCarty. She went on to start a ministry in each town we lived in, and all of them are still going strong today after 30 years.

The AstroDome was only ten minutes away, and I loved sitting with some of the old veterans and watching the Astros play. I listened to everything these heroes from the major leagues would say. There were all kinds of charity golf tournaments, and at the very first one I went to, I was supposed to be the celebrity for the group. A banker from Austin asked when the celebrity was going to show up. I didn't tell him I was the celebrity. I just said, "I don't know."

There were plenty of celebrity athletes in Houston and many made themselves available to talk to the team at FCA share times. George Foreman, Carl Lewis, and Evander Holyfield all lived in the area. One of my most embarrassing moments happened when Olympic gymnast Mary Lou Retton came to talk to the team. I had made up an honorary Rice football pass to give to her, and thought I had pulled it out of my pocket and handed it to her. After I gave it to her, she said, "Coach, why did you hand me the key to your hotel room?"

One the most meaningful FCA share times at Rice was a joint talk by Dave Rowe, a broadcaster for Ray Com and All Pro noseguard for the Raiders, and Bobby Maples, an All Pro center for the Broncos. They were longtime rivals from the AFL days. I remember the two of them hugging and in tears when they finished. Bobby was battling cancer. Years later, Dave Rowe would do another share time for my Lenoir Rhyne team in Hickory. Carey Casey, a dear friend and head of the inner city ministry for FCA in Dallas, also spoke at our share times. He had been Bob Trott's roommate at UNC so I had known him way back at Arkansas.

I had good personnel with me at Rice. Barbara Tolar, our administrative assistant, had been there ever since we had met when I had interviewed for the assistant's job at Rice years earlier. Her husband had been a great player for the Houston Oilers. Jackie Miles, the Rice equipment man, currently with the Carolina Panthers, was one of the best in the business. Allen Eggert was a great trainer and friend. Our strength coach was Keith Irwin, and his assistant was Jeff Madden. Now Jeff is an assistant AD with Mack Brown and is in charge of the entire strength program at Texas.

Jeff was instrumental in our success at Rice. When I was about to become the head coach, he flew to California and convinced Eric Henley to return to Rice. Eric became a great receiver and played a big part in many of the turnaround wins like Baylor and the U of A. When I had my back surgery in 1989, Jeff and his wife came to see me in Hermann hospital. I had no memory of it because of the morphine they were giving me. Five years later, we were all at a Christmas party in Durham. As soon as I saw them, I had a flashback to the hospital room and even remembered the bright orange dress Jeff's wife had been wearing.

I looked forward to starting a winning tradition and taught the team the Rice fight song a fan's dad had written in 1924. It was called "The Old Gray Bonnet". They were supposed to sing it every time they won. In 1989, we started Donald Hollas at quarterback. He was a tough kid and a leader. He became a NFL quarterback and played five or six years. Trevor Cobb also started. We won two games in 1989 and tied Wake Forest. Rice almost had that game won until the back judge called a 15 yard spearing penalty on O.J. Brigance. I was shocked to see that the judge was Doug Rhodes. Doug had been a fraternity brother of mine at Florida. Everyone thought he had died in Vietnam. Now he is the supervisor of officials for the ACC.

The night before my first game as a head coach, Jimmy Johnson, who was starting his first year as the Dallas Cowboys head coach, was staying in the same hotel, and we visited outside our meeting rooms. My first pregame interview as a head coach was also Craig James' first broadcast. The first game we played was SMU, right after SMU came off the death penalty. We beat them pretty badly and broke a 30 game losing streak.

Rice had a great player in OJ Brigance. No other SWC school offered him, but he was a special guy who was All Pro when he played in Canada seven years. He wanted to see if he had what it took to play in the NFL and asked if I could help him get a tryout with the Miami Dolphins. Weighing 215 lbs., he made the team and made the opening tackle in a Super Bowl, got cut, played with another team in the Super Bowl, worked for the Ravens, and then got ALS (Lou Gehrig's disease). He is fighting it and has a wonderful wife standing by him. They are strong Christians. His Rice team keeps up with him and we all got together recently for a reunion and fundraiser to fight ALS.

Before the U of A game, Brigance had a good idea about using the defense to practice against our offense instead of the scout team since we ran the same defense as Arkansas. He thought it would give them more realistic competition. He showed unselfish leadership knowing he would get no rest, but he thought it would make the team better. We did get better, but we didn't beat Arkansas even thought we were tied until late in the fourth quarter. During the game we lost Hollas to a broken leg. Willig came in and played well, but Arkansas' Derek Russell ran a reverse that gave the Hogs the win.

Some of the Arkansas players were mad that I was calling their plays, but most of the guys on my old team met me on the field after the game. That game helped the Owls get ready for a strong Baylor team that fielded four first round draft picks; we beat them 6-3. The Waco paper said, "It doesn't get any worse than this." Rice had been at the bottom of the conference for so long that it was hard for good teams to get up to play us. No one expected to lose to Rice. The next week Baylor bounced back and beat Texas 50-7. It was so long between our first win and when we finally beat Baylor in the tenth game that the team forgot the words to the fight song. We came close against Texas in Austin but lost 31-30 on a bad call. The kids played their hearts out, and that loss stung.

The next week we played the University of Houston. Andre Ware was announced as the Heisman trophy winner in the Rice team room. It was kind of embarrassing at the end of our humiliating loss.

The stage was set for a turnaround. The Athletic Review Committee at Rice was always talking about doing away with football; we needed to show Texas high school football coaches that Rice football was viable.

1990 was a better year. Morale was good. We changed the uniform to the more popular black shoes and had larger attendance at games. We had youth days and promotions to get groups like the Boy Scouts to come out and support Rice and give us more of a fan base since we only had 2,600 students. We also started a tradition of singing the fight song with the student section at the end of the game. We were gaining confidence, and when I gave pep talks before big games, I would tell my players, "Why not Rice?" We were starting to feel like winners, and we almost had a winning season in 1990.

Beating Arkansas 19-11 was a huge milestone for us. Hatfield had left and gone to Clemson under difficult circumstances. It meant so much to win with kicking and defense and win the Hatfield way. Trevor Cobb rushed for over 100 yards that day. Our victory in Little Rock was big for the whole Goldsmith family. Our daughter Kim and her husband Joel were living in Fayetteville, and Robin had come up from Austin College in TX. We also got to spend some time with Willeen McKennon. We went back to the hotel and Dick Hatfield and I watched Ken Hatfield's Clemson game together. It was a wonderful night for all the Rice coaches who had been together at Arkansas. We were all ecstatic, and I was so happy I couldn't quit crying.

Beating Arkansas in Little Rock was the highlight of my career.

The Houston game was close in the first half even though Houston was in the top 10 and had another Heisman quarterback in David Klinger. The game started at 9:30 p.m. Matt Sign said, "We won on Saturday and lost on Sunday because when the game ended Sunday at 12:45a.m. the score was 22-21."

Our record was 5-5 going into the Baylor game. It came down to the last play of the last game when we scored on a 30 yard Hail Mary against Baylor. It was before college football had overtime, so we could kick an extra point and tie, or go for the win to try to be 6-5. I was struggling because I wanted our team to get rid of the loser label. I asked Dinger what we could do for a two point play. Dave Cope, our tight end coach, had a good idea to try to draw them off sides. If they jumped, the Owls would get it at the one and a half yard line and could go for two. We called a play that would allow us to throw a quick pass or run Cobb. Instead of taking one step, the backup quarterback took three steps and got nailed in the back, so we lost the game. If Rice had won, we would have been eligible for a bid to the Independence Bowl.

After the 1990 season, they offered me a new contract at Rice. LSU called and said I was in their top four if I would interview with them. It was tempting because they had some good players, but I knew we were ready to compete at Rice, and I wanted to stay with the team. I told them, "There is a time when a coach's word needs to mean something. I gave Rice a commitment when I came here and they have reaffirmed their commitment to me."

In 1989, Bert Emanuel had been one of the top recruits in Houston. In 1990, he was at UCLA with Terry Donahue. Bert called me in the middle of the season wanting to come back to Houston. I called Terry. He promised me that if we didn't talk to Bert anymore during the season and Bert didn't change his mind, he would release him to us at the end of the season. Bert had lost the quarterback start to Tommy Maddox, but he could run a 4.28 forty yard dash and wanted to play for Rice. I thought I had done such a good job recruiting and that's why Bert wanted to come back home until I met his girlfriend and saw how beautiful she was. She probably was the real reason he wanted to come back. Bert said, "When I first talked to him, I knew he was a man who stuck to his word. It makes all the difference in the world to have a head coach on your side. He's the type of father-figure you want." Terry kept his word and Bert became a major factor in our success.

1991 started out promising, but the faculty committee at Rice wanted to do away with football. The Houston Post even ran a front page article about it. On March 7, 1991, the Board of Governors issued a decree of support for the football program, but obviously the controversy wasn't good for morale or recruiting. We still lacked depth at many positions and we were still using equipment managers on the scout team. Bert Emanuel arrived and was a great leader in the off season even though he was ineligible for that year. The Owls were off to a good start by beating Northwestern and they finally beat Tulane in the Super Dome after losing to them in '89 and '90.

The third game, Iowa State, was a heartbreaking loss. They were a good Big 8 team and we had put a whippin' on them most of the day with a great ground attack. Trevor was leading the nation in rushing yardage at the time, and had tons of rushing yards in the first two games. Rice had a 10 point lead with about two minutes to go. Trevor had gained 242 yards. All of the sudden I looked over and saw Cobb and the first team quarterback were not in the game. Rice had freshmen playing with the lead when our freshman tailback fumbled. Iowa State got the ball on their 35 and on third and 10 they hit a first down and hit a pass over the middle underneath the zone to score a touchdown. They went for two and made it, narrowing the lead to a two point lead. They got the onside kick and one first down. On the last play of the game they drilled a 48 yard field goal with no timeouts and won. I was furious at Dinger for taking the quarterback and the star running back out, but I wasn't going to throw Dinger under the bus at the press conference. Reporters asked why I took Trevor out, so I took the blame and told them I thought we had the game under control. Dinger more than made up for that mistake by the fantastic coaching job he did over the next four years.

Monday morning, Sports Illustrated named me as their Bonehead Coach of the Week. Texas whipped us by about three touchdowns the next week. Baylor had just upset the number one team, the University of Colorado, and Santana Dotson had blocked a Colorado field goal for a late fourth quarter win. We got behind in the first half against Baylor, but we fought back and forth driving and faced a 43 yard field goal into the wind. Chris Miller ran the fake and Santana Dotson, who started for the Packers a number of years later, came roaring in for the block. Chris ran 17 yards to get closer for a 27 yard field goal attempt. Darrell Richardson popped it in to win, and Rice got four wins that year.

After the 1991 season, we left the suburb of Sugar Creek and moved into the West U neighborhood to be close to Rice. There we started attending Tommy Clanton's Bible study. Clanton was a doctor who had been a former AFA player. We also switched to Second Baptist Church because it was closer to home.

Our pastor was Dr. Ed Young. Our son-in-law, Joel McDaniel and daughter joined us in Houston when Joel was hired as a youth pastor at Second Baptist Church.

In 1992, Tommy Hetherington, Trevor Cobb and Bert Emanuel were all more experienced. Larry Izzo, another undersized but smart player, came in as a freshman. We didn't have our pick of the cream of the crop, and only Minnesota and Rice offered him. By that time Jim Wacker, who had been the coach at TCU and was familiar with Izzo, was the coach at

Minnesota. Before the 92 season, I looked at all the recruits on tape again and Izzo was the best one. Larry played for the Woodlands against Emory Bellard, the coach who had invented the wishbone when he was on Darrell Royal's staff. Izzo was the best player on the field, and he played both ways. In Larry's freshman year he made a huge play for us by battling against the number one recruit in Texas and intercepting the ball, enabling us to upset Texas Tech. He was a key figure for us in breaking the losing streak in 1992.

Rice played the USAFA in our opening game, and I thought I would be real smart and have Bert be the personal protector on the punt so they wouldn't dare rush that punt, but he wasn't a tough blocker. They blocked it for a touchdown and we lost by one point. That was Bert's first game. Josh LaRocca was still the starter.

The Duke game started well, but the momentum changed after the game was delayed by lightning and LaRocca broke his collarbone. Rice went down 13-0. Bert Emanuel came in there and brought the Owls back up to the last play when the receiver dropped the ball, or Rice would have won.

Bert started the next game. I thought Dinger putting together an offense that Emanuel could execute, a quick hitting passing game for short yardage, was the greatest coaching job I had ever seen. After that we started beating tough teams.

We battled tooth and nail on a hot day in October and barely lost to Texas 23-21 on a controversial call. In the second half, Bert Emanuel was having a field day and the big UT linemen couldn't keep up with him. We were down by two points with two minutes to go. Unfortunately the clock wasn't on our side and we didn't get the onsides kick. Kurt Roper looked like a great receiver pulling that ball in and keeping his foot in bounds. It was a great play but the officials didn't give it to him .We ran out of time, but we were the best team that day.

Kurt was the last one recruited in 1990. His team had won the state championship in OK. He didn't fit our offense at QB, but his dad had coached at Texas A&M and Arkansas and had played on the U of A national championship team. We gave him our last scholarship because we knew he was a winner. We ended up with better quarterbacks, and we backed down some on promising him a lot of playing time, but he said he would come no matter what and prove he could play in the SWC. We kept our commitment to him and he kept his commitment to us. He got to Rice and couldn't throw like the other quarterbacks. He called a timeout in our first practice and said, "Coach, don't you think it's time for you to move me to defense; I'm no quarterback." I didn't want to break his heart by moving him the first day, but he was a coach's kid and knew what would be best for the team

In the tenth ball game, Rice had the chance to get the first winning season in 30 years at Navy. Dal Shealy did our chapel. Dal had been there for the Miracle on the Brazos as offensive coordinator when Baylor and Grant Teaff won the SWC conference for the first time in 50 years. The game was suspended in the third quarter for a tornado watch, and it rained so hard it felt like we were playing in a monsoon. Navy had the momentum when I felt a tap on my shoulder. Shealy had an idea to help the struggling offense. He said, "They are pursuing hard to the ball Fred; do you have a misdirection play?" The very next play Dinger called a misdirection play. Emanuel pitched the ball underneath to Jimmy Lee who went 55 yards for the touchdown. Dal said, "I gotta catch a plane; you finish it up." We won the game, broke our 30 year losing streak, and our fans tore down the goalposts.

My most joyous memory during the celebration was Pam hugging me in the tunnel outside our locker room and seeing the bright smile on her face. We had worked together for this moment for many years. Holding my beautiful bride and seeing that smile made the struggles worthwhile. She was our best recruiter and was always in that tunnel for me, the players, and their parents, win or lose.

We were competitive with Texas A&M as well. The score was 14-7 midway through the third quarter, and they tipped a pass to win the game. We beat TCU, Texas Tech, and Baylor. Baylor was undefeated, eighth in the nation, and heavily favored. Late in the game Rice kicked a field goal to go up by three, and on Baylor's last drive, Shane Hollas stopped Baylor All American fullback Robert Straight on fourth and inches to win the game. At the end of the season, we got beat by Houston to knock us out of a bowl. Cobb concluded a fine career in which he gained

4,948 rushing yards to become the second leading rusher in SWC history. It was a wonderful feeling to go 6-5 and get that first winning season. Bert Emanuel, Jimmy Lee, and Matt Sign earned All Conference honors. Trevor Cobb won the Doak Walker Award and signed with the Kansas City Chiefs. The Rice staff was so proud to be a part of taking the team from nothing and turning them into winners in four years.

In 1993 our time at Rice was beginning to wind down. It would prove to be our last season there. Not looking to leave, my goal was to have another winning season and try to get to a bowl. In January, we had been in Atlanta at the coaching convention. Pam and I drove to North Point Mall and had lunch with Ken and Sandy Hatfield. I remember feeling too prideful, but it made me feel good at lunch hearing Pam tell them that Sports Illustrated had named me the Sports Illustrated National NCAA Coach of the Year. It wasn't like Pam to brag about anything, so it meant a lot to hear her say that.

Flying into Houston, the Rice AD called and said we had to raise some money. He wanted to play the University of Arizona. They had a desert storm defense that was stomping everyone, and I didn't think our offense would do well against them. I didn't want to play for money, but if we had to, I wanted more money and a bigger name. We got a TV game against John Cooper and future Heisman winner Eddie George's Ohio State team and made about $500,000. We lost 34-7. Our chapel speaker that day was two time Heisman winner Archie Griffin. He has played for my boss from FAMU, Rudy Hubbard, so it was a thrill to hear him speak.

At the beginning of the 1993 season, we also gained a good recruit we thought we had lost. Brendan Goin, a big 6'4" 225 lb noseguard with good grades, had picked West Point over all the big names. We had already started summer practice and Goin used the first call he could make from basic training to ask me for a scholarship. He was in great shape after boot camp at West Point. Goin started and made a huge impact right away and became an all time sack leader for Rice.

Bert made a prediction that we would win our last three games, and it fired Baylor up. The Baylor game was a close game; that day the wind was bad, and we stayed a touchdown behind them and couldn't catch up. Our last game was on national TV against the University of Houston the day after Thanksgiving. We finally beat Kim Helton's team. He is a great coach who had a successful five year stint at the U of H and went on to coach four NFL teams. Though they were our rivals, Pam and I became good friends with Kim and his wife Pam. That was also the case with most of the SWC coaches and wives. We enjoyed socializing with the Slocums, Teaffs, Dykes, McWilliams, Greggs, Wackers, and Sullivans. Later I ended up hiring Kim's oldest son, Clay, at Duke. Now Clay coaches at Southern Cal. I was so glad Helton threw out the run and shoot offense that Jack Pardee had run because we couldn't have stopped that. We won the Bayou Bucket which was always awarded to the winner of our annual rivalry. We ended 1993 with back to back winning seasons and went 6-5 again. At 6-5 we weren't bowl eligible because one of our wins had been against a 1AA team.

Duke Blue Devils

We were happy at Rice. We had had two winning seasons, and I loved the kids, but our facilities were horrendous and Baylor's new Kasey Center was better. SMU and TCU were also upgrading. Our locker room had little rows of cubby holes. Rice had a small weight room, and the stadium had old wooden seats that were falling apart. I started a drive to replace them with aluminum seats. At the same time Duke was calling because their coach, Barry Wilson, had resigned, I was promised that the facilities would be improved by some members of the Rice Board of Trustees. I was also troubled by rumblings of the SWC falling apart.

Overall, I wasn't looking for a job, although Rice was a tougher job than Duke because of the size of the city, competition with the pro teams, and the competition against Texas and Texas A&M for recruits and fan support. Duke had more of a name brand and alumni support. Rice only had 2,600 students. There wasn't a lot of local support; they didn't have the resources to extend the brand that Duke had. At one time I had considered the Duke job because I felt like Duke could recruit anywhere and I didn't think as much of the ACC as the SWC. I thought it would be easier except for FSU, but I had decided I wasn't interested. At our football banquet, I told the team that I had no intention of going to Duke.

In 1993 Pam and I flew to NYC to see Buddy Dial, a Rice alum, inducted into the National Football Hall of Fame. We had a wonderful time and saw old coaching friends like the Spurriers, and I ran into a high school teammate, Ron Pantello. Pam and I took a taxi from the Waldorf to Brooklyn, found where my grandparents had lived, and rode through Prospect Park where Aunt Ruth and Uncle Jack used to take me out on rowboats and buy me Cracker Jacks. Then we went to Ebbets Field and saw where the Dodgers had played. I hadn't been back there since I was six.

When we got back to Houston, we took the Allshouses to a party and found Rice was putting the new facilities plan on hold because they didn't want to upset the Rice faculty since some still wanted to do away with football. It irritated me to find out it was put on hold. That week I went to Dallas recruiting and had heard on the radio that Duke had hired the football coach from William and Mary, Jim Laycock. I was recruiting at Coach Mike Sneed's school, Colleyville High School in Grapevine, TX, and I told him that I wasn't going anywhere. I got back in the car and called Duke to congratulate them on hiring a coach. They told me the other coach had changed his mind.

The secretary put Tom Butters on the phone and he put a hard sell on for reconsidering Duke. I really started thinking about it and flew back to

Houston. Saturday we had a Christmas party with our staff. I had already given them all the reasons why we weren't going to Duke. Pam and I stayed up late talking about it. Our daughter, Pam's sister, and some dear friends lived in Houston. Pam was happy in Houston and there were many reasons to stay put.

On Sunday morning our Sunday school teacher talked about Deuteronomy 30 and going back to the land of your forefathers. Pam's ancestors had immigrated to Western Carolina from Scotland, and she had relatives in North Carolina. We thought that was interesting, but we still went to bed that night with the idea of staying at Rice.

At about four the next morning, I jolted awake and felt like the Lord was telling me I was prepared for Duke after being at Air Force and Rice. I got ready to fly to Durham. I already knew the flight schedule. I decided to call Tom Butters; if he was there and wanted me to interview, I'd come. I dressed up in a suit and woke Pam up. She gave me her blessing and I left. I started calling on the way to the airport. Normally I parked in an outlying lot at the airport, but I got a parking place right by the door. That was a miracle in itself to get that place. I couldn't get Tom on the phone and went inside and called from a phone booth- still no answer. I got the ticket and decided not to go if I couldn't get Butters. He still didn't answer, so I refunded the ticket, and decided to call one more time from the car. It was about 7:30a.m. in Durham. Lynn Butters had had the phone turned off all night, and when she turned the phone back on it was ringing.

She said, "I know Tom wants you to be his football coach; he'll be ecstatic, just come on!"

I got another ticket, ran to the first gate, jumped on the plane and flew to Durham. Barry Wilson, who had recently resigned as the Duke head coach, picked me up at the airport. We were longtime friends and it was special to me that he would do that. He said it would take a great coaching job to have any kind of defense with these guys. He probably would have been right, but Jamal Ellis's return after missing the '93 season, and John Zuanich's return after shoulder surgery were a huge help. Ray Farmer, Billy Granville, and Bernard Holsey all matured into fine pro prospects as juniors. Two years later all of them were drafted to the NFL and had four to ten year careers. Craig Bohl's pressure defense was also new to the ACC.

Barry dropped me off at Tom's house. It was a warm day in Durham, so we talked outside. His wife wouldn't let Tom smoke cigars so he hid one out in a tree by the patio, the same way he did at the office. I told him I felt like the Lord wanted me to be in Durham. I said, "I am Jewish and I am also a Christian and I will share my faith with the football team. If you have any objections, tell me now." Then he took a puff on his cigar, and said, "I want you to be my coach." Some of the things I asked for, like two dealer cars, Duke hadn't done before, so Butters had to ask the president for them. On the flight home, a Duke football player, Ray Wright, told me about one of his teammates, Jamal Ellis. Jamal wasn't planning on coming back, but I got his number and we talked him into coming back.

There were huge differences between Duke and Rice. I ran into Steve Hatchell, Commissioner of the Southwest Conference, in the Houston Hobby airport. He said I ought to go to Duke because the conference was going to dissolve in a year or two and Rice would be left out. The next year was the last year of the SWC and Rice shared the championship with four teams, but all the big name schools got out and Rice ended up in the WAC. I went back to Dallas the next day to recruit and later on that day Rice had a new contract for me. I had asked for two year contracts for all my Rice assistants as well. The same day, Butters called and met all my requirements and asked me to come to Durham for another interview.

While I was at Duke interviewing, Ken Hatfield happened to call Pam, and she told him where I was. He didn't think I should take the job, but he had just been fired by Clemson and wanted the Rice job if I decided to leave. I flew from Dallas to Houston to tell the Rice coaches. We had to decide what coaches to take or leave behind. The next morning the Butters picked Pam and me up. We checked into the Washington Duke and then met with Nan Keohane, Duke's president. There was no vote. Tom just called the search committee together to tell them they were hiring me. I called Rice AD Bobby May and gave him Hatfield's name for the Rice job. I told him, "You lose the pupil but you can get the mentor." Dinger would have gotten the Rice job it if it hadn't been for Ken. I had to recommend Ken because he was my best friend, but I always felt guilty for Dinger not getting the job even though he ended up with a successful career in pro football.

I was able to bring six of my coaches to Duke and hired Rod Broadway, Jimmy Gonzales, and Fred Chatham. I wish I had found a place on the staff for Ted Roof because he had been a good recruiter for Duke in Atlanta. Shirley and Mary were wonderful administrative assistants for our football offices. They were staying until 9:00p.m.during recruiting and finally came in and asked if they still had jobs. No one had let them know if they were staying or not.

Bobby Trott remembers the condition of the football offices:

> Duke hadn't invested in technology for the football program. They had a lot of old office supplies. Even the hole punches didn't work. It bugged me, so I piled them up in front of Fred's office door so he'd order new ones. They didn't even have answering machines and we were missing weekend calls. The old dot matrix printer took two hours to run scouting reports and Shirley had an outdated computer. She was the last to get a new one, and she was so thankful she cried when she got it. The office had old recycled white boards that didn't line up. One was 6' and one was 8' with a gap in the middle. I complained about them, and Fred told me to quit griping about that gap and

just worry about the gap in the defense. He was born to coach. He can remember every game. Together we made a good pair. We went through good times and hard times, but most were good times.

At my first team meeting I wore an army fatigue hat and told the players they were going into battle to play for Duke. I told them to be ready for off season conditioning the first day they returned after Christmas break. On that first day of conditioning, I hit the Duke track to run at 5:30 in the morning. I wanted to show the players I wasn't asking them to do anything I hadn't done. I had heard one of the players had an attitude problem, and I wanted to motivate him, so I told him I would run with him. I was 50 and had already run once that day.

When I was walking out after meeting with the team, I heard some of them complaining. Patrick Manley told them to shut up… he wasn't about to go 3-8 again and would do whatever the coaches wanted. He maintained a strong work ethic. As of 2012, Patrick Manley has played for the Chicago Bears longer than any other player, including Walter Payton. Zaid Aleem was another leader on the team. He decided to return to play even though he could have graduated. Zaid was an impressive young man who spoke seven languages and started out making six figures with Morgan Stanley immediately after graduation. At our first spring practice, we were disappointed to find out Rice had had more talent than Duke, but some of the players were ready for a change. Robert Baldwin wanted to get serious. He called me and said, "Don't give up on me. I'll be back in shape." He would go on to be the ACC Player of the Year.

There were some wonderful people associated with Duke. Dr. Leroy Walker had been the Chairman of the Olympic Committee, and he was always in our press box cheering us on. Crash Davis, the baseball player that inspired the movie Bull Durham, and Country Ennis Slaughter, a famous Cardinal, were loyal fans. One of the most special gifts I received at Duke was a beautiful blue and white carpet from Ace Parker. As of 2012, Ace is 100 years old and is the oldest living NFL player. Ace was a Duke football player who also played Major League baseball.

We enjoyed watching Coach K's basketball team and the school spirit at Duke. I even served hot dogs to the Cameron Crazies. Pam and I enjoyed our first NCAA basketball tournament in Greensboro. Sylvia Hatchell, UNC's head women's basketball coach attended our Sunday school class at Cresset Baptist Church, as did Carl Torbush, the UNC head football coach. I was probably the only Duke employee rooting for Carolina when one of Sylvia's players made the game winning shot to win the Women's National Championship. The next season she took some flak at Carolina for doing a FCA share time for our Duke football team. They found out about it because when Ray Farmer blocked a kick to win a game for us, he told the paper that her pep talk had inspired him. She had shown them how a group of sticks bound together was stronger than sticks by themselves. After watching the women's game on TV at the hotel, we made it to the coliseum in time to watch the Arkansas-Florida game. It had been a long wait for everyone else because President Clinton was there and security was beefed up, but we were able to walk right in at halftime.

When we got on the elevator in the hotel, Sandy Koufax, a Brooklyn Dodger who was one of my heroes, and Jaleel White, Urkel on *Family Matters*, were in there with us. I told Jaleel I liked Urkel because he always made me laugh on Friday nights before a game. We got to see Nolan Richardson, Tony Cherico and Raven Caldwell from the University of Arkansas and watch Arkansas beat Duke to win the National Championship. That spring was also my first introduction to the Valvano Kids Classic which I had the opportunity to co-chair with Pam Valvano, and also the Duke Children's Classic. Perry Como celebrated his eightieth birthday in Cameron Indoor Stadium at the Duke Children's Classic. Rich Little did a show, and I had a chance to have dinner with Carl Eskine. Bob Harris, our Duke broadcaster, knew Clem Lebine, another Dodger hero, so we got to play golf with him during the Children's Classic.

In addition to raising money through the Duke Children's Classic, we had the opportunity to spend time with the children who had come to Duke for medical treatment. The Ronald McDonald house was near our campus and some of the children surprised us by bringing oranges to our practice one day. I was proud of the way our players made them feel special and took the time to play with them. The kickers helped the little boys kick with them, and Spence Fischer and Ray Farmer let a little girl named Nicole try on their helmets and throw the football with them. Their supervisor, Michael Gagnon, said in *THE CHRONICLE*:

> All of this was unannounced. It was spontaneous on the part of Goldsmith and his team. They were having as much fun as the kids were having. They knelt down to put themselves on eye level and asked our kids about their schools and what towns they were from. That day we were surrounded by champions led by a champion of hearts in Goldsmith. Our little Nicole soaked in the attention and beamed like a lighthouse. This was her last birthday. She died three months later. Thanks to Goldsmith and his team, our kids had their day in the sun and lived some dreams that life would not give them the opportunity to experience later. No parent could have wished for such a gift. This kind of thing does not show up on the win- loss column, not down here on Earth anyway.

I was enjoying the atmosphere at Duke. I knew it had a reputation for being a basketball school, but after attending the basketball games, I didn't see why we couldn't get the students to support football as well. To generate excitement, I sent letters to all 1600 Duke freshmen asking them to support the team. We wanted to show our fans we appreciated their support, so we started a tradition of going over to the stands and taking our helmets off while the band played the alma mater after the game. We had borrowed that tradition from the University of Texas when we played them at Rice. To improve our chances of starting a winning program, we also established a good rapport with admissions and added Western Carolina and Northwestern to the schedule.

We were scared to death to start football because Duke didn't look as good as Rice had been. I got frustrated with the team in spring practice because all they wanted to do was fight with each other. I told them I wouldn't put up with that; that's how losers acted. Duke had a good quarterback in Spence Fischer, but we didn't have a good running back. We weren't sure about the receivers. We had some key players returning: Baldwin, Ellis, Farquar, Khayat, Farmer, and Aleem. I was starting to feel pretty confident in our offense, but the day before football season started, Chatham asked Dinger if it would work. He said, "How the heck should I know? We've never done it before." We brought a different kind of offense and defense that was all new to the ACC. Dinger had gotten it from Shanahan.

The Sunday school lesson we had studied in Houston right before we moved was from Deuteronomy 6. It tells the Israelites that when God brings them back to the land that belonged to their fathers they are to honor, obey, and love God with all their hearts and it will go well with them, and that they will multiply and prosper in the land. Those first few years, we felt like those verses applied to our family, that God had led us to North Carolina, and that he was blessing us. During our time at Duke, our family increased. Robin moved to North Carolina and married Clint Park, a GA at Duke with us, and my daughter Kim had twins, Kinsey and Kayla. It was unheard of to have no injuries in 12 games of college football, but that is exactly what happened in 1994.

We opened with a TV game vs. Maryland. We had 25,000 in attendance. They were a good team. They ran the run and shoot and had had all kinds of passing records in the ACC the year before. We put Ellis on the #1 receiver in the ACC (who would be an All Pro receiver later), and put everyone else in the zone. Ellis shut down the receiver, Baldwin gained 240 yards, quarterback Spence Fischer ripped them apart, and Thomas caught a bunch of touchdown passes. The next game, we beat ECU by stopping them on fourth down when Billy Granville blitzed the quarterback and knocked the ball down to win 13-12 in front of 35,000 at home. I told Butters that if we could beat them we would be good enough to go to a bowl game. He thought I was crazy.

The Army game was on ESPN on a Thursday night. We won big, 43-7, against a good Army team. They even accused me of running up the score. Our redshirt freshman, David Green, was the backup quarterback that day. Late in the game, he recognized the coverage from the game plan and executed it just like we had taught him in practice. He didn't realize he wasn't supposed to run the score up; he was just excited to score twice in his first game. I took the heat for that in the media. After that game, Lee Corso said, "You need to get the hell outta here after this season. Remember what happened to me at Indiana."

Our fourth game was Georgia Tech. We were excited to play. They had an open date the week before and had some injuries and came in flat. This game was significant to me because we were playing on hallowed ground at Grant Field in Bobby Dodd Stadium. Everybody wanted to go to Georgia Tech when I was growing up, but I didn't have the grades or the talent to go there. I was pinching myself to think I could coach a game there as the head coach of Duke University. Spence Fischer and a lot of our guys were from Atlanta, so they were excited to play at home. Dinger and Les Koenning worked well together. We had brought the one back West Coast passing game to the East Coast. Dinger was a great innovator. He decided we wouldn't have any backs in the backfield and called it the Tech formation. We moved Baldwin to wide receiver and the corners had to cover him. Back then, Dinger was doing so much of what we see in college football today out of necessity.

We were playing decent when we had a third and long in the second quarter. I decided to do a quick kick. Fischer punted the ball to the one yard line. Then Tech couldn't get out of the hole. We made them punt and drove down and scored. When they kicked off, John Zawanich got a turnover. Craig Bohl's great defense and the quick kick all contributed to our win. That was the turning point that gave us a 17 point lead, and we went on to a big upset. I was so excited, I ran off the field yelling Woo Pig Sooie. It was kind of embarrassing when a Sports Illustrated reporter heard me and put that in his article. I had forgotten that the Hogs had beaten Duke in the NCAA basketball championship that year.

By the Navy game, more Sports Illustrated reporters were covering us, and Duke started letting us fly instead of riding a bus. Coach K hated Navy because he was an Army grad, and he got our team fired up to play them. It was pouring down rain and we were stuck in horrible traffic when we got to the D.C. area. I felt sorry for our police escorts. My friend from the Arkansas staff, Richard Bell, was Navy's defensive coordinator. I knew we were favored, and they were struggling. I told Bohl to blitz them almost every play. We played hard and didn't allow ourselves to get cocky. We won 47-14 and were featured in Sports Illustrated.

We were completely sold out for Clemson. It was an important game to me because they were considered a power in the league and had fired my friend Ken Hatfield the year before. It was a close game, but towards the end, Ray Farmer blocked a punt and Corey Thomas scooped it up for a touchdown. They drove down to the 35 and had to have a touchdown on fourth and six to win. We called a blitz. I was just praying it would work. Zaid Aleen hit the quarterback in the backfield to win the game. Bohl yelled "That dog will hunt!" And we were 6-0.

We put a hurting on Wake Forest. The first five times they had the ball our defense caused turnovers, and we won by at least 50 points. Lamar Marshall had a good game in his hometown. He is now one of the top coaches in N.C. We were 7-0 and Bob Harris started introducing me as The Coach of the Undefeated Blue Devils on our TV show. They hadn't been as successful since Duke went to a bowl game in 1989.

We had an open date the next week and I spoke to the Tallahassee Quarterback Club. I had the pleasure of sitting on the platform next to a young FSU assistant named Mark Richt. He told me about their great players,

Warrick Dunn and Derrick Brooks. When Pam and I watched the FSU-Miami game on TV she said, "Do we really have to play them next week?"

Florida State was still undefeated when we met, and we were tied for first place in the ACC. Our game was billed as the championship for the ACC. I remember standing out on the field with Dinger and it made our Gator blood boil when they started the Tomahawk chop. I told Dinger I'd give anything to be able to be able to play the Gators against them instead of Duke. Burt Reynolds had played for FSU and was out there standing beside me in a Seminole outfit when the mascot threw the spear down right beside me. I was already mad, and that irritated me even more. We were only behind 14-6 five minutes before the half. They scored and got a turnover, and just like that it was 35-6 at the half. It reminded me of the feeling I had once when Arkansas was getting killed by Miami at halftime. They beat us 50-24, but we fought back and scored a lot of points in the second half. I felt like we had played them even that half. I was proud of our guys. We were knocking on the door of the top 10 at 7-1.

Virginia had the Barber twins when we played them, and they were a strong favorite. The quarterback was Michael Groh. His dad, Al, had coached with us at the USAFA. When we had our walk through the day before the game, I told the seniors not to be afraid; Virginia was just an academic school like us. I asked how in the world they could be worried about not beating Virginia.

The crowd was standing room only. They got off to a lead and we went back and forth hitting Khayat and Farquar with some big passes and pulling out a trick play we had used at Rice multiple times. We had tried it in the Army game, and London had dropped the ball and said he would never run that play on TV again. We threw it to Matt Diorio who made a diving catch in the end zone for the lead. Our true freshman, LeVance McQueen, picked off a pass and we ran the time out to win the game. We were 8-1 and close to the top 10 in the polls.

We came into N.C. State with injuries that affected the outcome of the game. Baldwin had turf toe and Tommy Cochran, our kicker, had a groin injury. We went ahead 23-7, but they hit an 80 yard bomb in the third quarter and kept breaking big plays. Cochran missed four field goals. The last drive of the game we were one point behind with less than two minutes to play when we got a first and ten at State's 15 yard line. We were in easy field goal range and got a holding call that put us back to the 30. The center had held a little bit, but not enough to justify the call. It was the only holding call of the game. We missed the 50 yard field goal attempt.

We played UNC the last game of the season. It was our homecoming and the attendance was 41,000. We were over capacity and tickets were sold out. A booster from Wilmington had traveled to Durham for the game and had to watch it on TV. I thought we had the better team even though they had a bunch of pro players and went on to beat Texas in their bowl game. Our offense did well but we couldn't put it away. We took the lead, but pooch kicked the kickoff, and they ran it back for a touchdown. Late in the game we regained the lead and kicked off with less than three minutes to go. We were outplaying them and had them down on their 20. After we dropped an interception, they hit Octavius Barnes on third and 9, and Pollock and Farmer missed the tackles. Barnes went 79 yards and scored and they went up 41-38. We got into position for a field goal to tie 41-41. We didn't have overtime yet, so I thought a tie could send us to the Cotton Bowl to play Texas Tech. We got to their 20 and threw a route we'd been doing well with all day. Spence was supposed to go to Khayat or Jensen if Khayat was covered. At the last second, the guy let Khayat go and came up to play Jensen and broke the ball up. Their linebacker dove for the ball and caught it. UNC hit Jensen well before the ball got there, so there should have been a pass interference call. Ironically, I had talked to the officials at their meeting at the Hilton that morning and told them games shouldn't be decided by a penalty at the end of the game if it could change the outcome. Bradley Faircloth, the supervisor of officials, agreed and they didn't call it. I had no one to blame but myself. They got the ball back and we held them for two downs. Then they took a safety and made the final score 41-40. The crowd got their money's worth; it was one of the all-time great thrillers. Everyone in the stadium was drained at the end of the game.

Pam and I walked into the basketball game that night and the whole crowd gave us a standing ovation. We were disappointed to miss the opportunity to go to the Cotton Bowl, but the Hall of Fame Bowl invited us and it was a warm, fun location for the guys. It was Duke's second bowl game in 30 years. The last time they had been to a bowl was in 1989 when Spurrier was their head coach. We played a great Wisconsin team that had won the Rose Bowl the year before. We had a wonderful time in Tampa, other than the game. The players got to ride around in a limo, and I got to sing the FAMU fight song with some of their band members who happened to be in Tampa, and I rode the Kumba roller coaster. UNC's famous four sport letterman Albert Long traveled with us and did our FCA share time along with Zenan Andrewshisson, the local FCA director and former Miami Dolphin kicker.

Wisconsin had finished in the top five in the nation the year before our bowl game against them and won the Rose Bowl the year before and the year after they played us. Our friend Scott Brown was on the Minnesota staff that had beaten Wisconsin that year, and he shared a plan to stop their offense. It was a new type of low risk efficient offense that Northwestern would later use to make their comeback in the big 10. We were also hoping the heat would give us an advantage. We started in a two minute offense to hurry up and get them tired. They were huge and physical, and it didn't work right away. The first two times we had the ball, we threw interceptions and they got a quick 13 point lead. We started coming back when their big defensive linemen got worn down. By the end of the third quarter it was a 13-13 game. They should have been killing us. We got down 20-13 in the fourth and gambled everything that they were going to run the ball right up the middle on fourth and one. They ran off tackle and bounced it out 40 yards for a touchdown to make it 27-13. The final score was 34-21. John Jensen suffered a severe knee injury on the last play of the game and could have lost his leg if he hadn't been rushed into surgery.

One of my most memorable players from the 1994 team is Brian Krenzel. I got to see Brian while we were at Lenoir Rhyne. Brian has put his Duke education to good use. He is an orthopaedic surgeon in Hickory, NC, and even though he wasn't Pam's doctor when she had a knee replacement at his hospital, he took good care of her by bringing her Starbucks coffee. Krenzel said:

> I thank God every day for the opportunity Coach Goldsmith gave me at Duke University. A Catholic kid from a three auto factory hometown doesn't typically get to experience a place like Duke. Coach encouraged me to use Duke and the relationships to think bigger and do more. More importantly, he showed me how to have a more personal relationship with Jesus Christ. Without a doubt, Coach Goldsmith and Duke gave me more in life than I could ever have given Duke University on the football field.

Brian asked me to include his version of some of the following conversations in this book:

BK: (after freshman year) Coach, what do I need to do to get better?

FG: (long pause) Hmmm. (another long pause) Well it's a good thing you are a fine student because you need to improve a lot as a football player.

BK: Really, Coach? You made this decision after one redshirt season?

FG: Been doing this awhile. I think you could be a fine doctor one day. You are a nice young man and a good Christian boy. As a football player, I like your chances better as a student.

BK: Good thing you are a nice Christian man, sir. As a coach, I like your chances better as a preacher one day. (He gave me a crooked grin and sent me on my way)

Brian says:

I think that moment changed our relationship as he saw me as a young man wanting to fight for a position and not simply as a homesick kid. When my senior year rolled around, I was starting to see some significant playing time. During the Monday practice before FSU (back when FSU was still FSU), we had the following conversation:

FG: Brian, come on over here.

BK: Yes, sir.

FG: You're gonna start Saturday.

BK: Against FSU?

FG: That's who we're playing.

BK: Someone injured?

FG: You wanna play or not?

BK: Sir, let me get this straight. I've been here three and a half years and haven't started a single game, not even Sisters of the Poor and now I'm good enough to start against FSU?

FG: That's right.

BK: You want me to run for president next week too?

Brian continues:

> A funny thing happened, I played well and
> played even better the next week against
> Virginia and caused a fumble. Then I recovered
> a fumble against Wake Forest the next week.
> Finally I scored a touchdown on a blocked punt
> against UNC in my last game. I was done. I
> was on time to graduate in four years and was
> going to start my medical education. I found
> great satisfaction in the fact that Coach
> recruited me harder to stay for my fifth year
> and be a captain than I had been recruited to
> come to Duke in the first place.
>
> The best story, however, is the gene pool story.
> When my brother Craig was a junior in high
> school, he was a big recruit. He was
> considering Duke along with many other
> schools. He ultimately chose Ohio State
> University – a great decision for him as he
> ended up 24-2 as the starting quarterback with
> a perfect season and a national championship
> under his belt. Craig was in the same recruiting
> class as Eli Manning and Chris Sims (both sons
> of legendary pro quarterbacks). Eli's older
> brother Peyton wasn't too bad either. Anyway,
> I was sitting in Coach Goldsmith's office about
> an hour after my brother called to tell me about
> his commitment when Coach Goldsmith
> strolled by.

FG: Brian, what are you doing here? You coming back to play?

Coach DeLamielleure: No, Coach, great news, his brother Craig committed to Ohio State.

FG: (Looks my way, a bit disappointed, like he wondered how I let this happen) Brian, he's a smart boy like you. He should have come to Duke.

BK: Knowing the recruiting board in his office ranked the quarterbacks: 1. Manning 2. Sims 3. Krenzel, I jokingly said, "Coach Cooper told Craig he was their #1 guy. He went where he felt the love. Why #3 on your board, Coach?"

FG: (In classic deadpan fashion) I looked at Eli's daddy and brother, I looked at Sim's Daddy, and then I looked at your brother's family tree. Well ... I went with the gene pool.

We had many character kids like Brian, and I thought we had a real chance to turn the program around. For the first time since 1943, we had three All Americans in the same year. They were: running back Robert Baldwin, who also earned ACC Player of the Year honors, free safety Ray Farmer, and offensive tackle Matt Williams. John Zawana led the ACC in tackles for losses. I was blessed to win the Bobby Dodd Coach of the Year award and the AFCA Region I Coach of the Year award. I turned down overtures from Miami, LSU, Oklahoma, and Michigan State because I had made a commitment to Tom Butters, the parents, the players, and my coaches, and I would not consider leaving Duke. Butters gave me another five year contract and had plans to upgrade our facilities. Albert Long remembers Tom telling him and Bucky Waters that first season, "One of the two best decisions I ever made at Duke, if not the best decision, I ever made was hiring Fred Goldsmith."

I stayed at Duke, but we lost both our coordinators after the bowl game. Craig Bohl went to Nebraska, and Dinger went to the Denver Broncos. Bohl stayed on for several years at Nebraska and won the Division IAA national championship at North Dakota State University in 2011. Dinger won two Super Bowls with the Broncos. They had been with me six years, and they weren't easy to replace. I tried to get Gary Crowton, a coordinator from Georgia Tech. He would have been perfect, but he had just been hired by Louisiana Tech and wouldn't go back on his word.

Our Cinderella season made recruiting easier. Billy Reed, a baseball legend and former quarterback at FAMU, helped recruit Dee Clark. Gannon Shepherd had played football and basketball in high school. His mother wasn't sure if she wanted him to continue playing football in college because he was already a big man at 6'8" 260 lbs., and she was worried about him getting too big. He ended up playing five years for the Jacksonville Jaguars. Gannon is married to Tim Tebow's sister now. Ryan Stodemeyer was getting all sorts of offers from the Big 10. His parents wanted him to play for Duke because his older brother Mike played on our team, so they asked me to fly out to his football banquet. I surprised him and told him I had spent

$600.00 on a plane ticket because we needed a great linebacker like him. Richmond Flowers, Scottie Montgomery, and Octavius Wilkes all would become great playmakers for us.

I found the ideal quarterback in Alabama. Spencer Romine was a straight A student from a wonderful Christian family. We battled Georgia Tech and Auburn for him, but he wanted to be a doctor so Duke was a good fit. When he was healthy, he quarterbacked the Northwestern victory. Unfortunately he was injured most of the time. I was disappointed for him because he was such a good quarterback.

Lenny Friedman was from a Jewish family who ran a camp for underprivileged kids in New York. Their claim to fame was that Whoopi Goldberg had been one of their campers. Notre Dame was also battling for Lenny, but I could say the Hebrew Shema and the Notre Dame coaches couldn't do that. Lenny ended up playing for us and having a long career in the NFL.

Chris Combs, Dawud Rasheed, Brian McCormick, Scottie Montgomery, Twambi Settles and Richmond Flowers also signed with us. Seven players from that 1995 class played in the NFL.

I thought Richmond had changed his mind later on. He called me really upset his first weekend on campus, and I thought he was going to say he was leaving Duke. When he told me he had gotten a DWI, we met in my office and called his father. His dad had me take his car keys away. I had to be hard on him, but

I was secretly ecstatic that he wasn't quitting the team. Richmond turned out to be a dream to coach. Later, he was the most valuable player in the Blue Gray All Star game before moving on to the NFL.

Mike Hart remembers recruiting and his host Scottie Montgomery. "I could tell the other places didn't have the camaraderie Duke did. They enjoyed and respected each other. Coach Goldsmith made a point to visit with my grandparents. They told me, 'Don't marry the woman you love, marry the woman that loves you.'"

1995 would be a losing season. I felt like we had seen the Deuteronomy 6 scripture, "The Lord your God will make you most prosperous in the works of your hand and fruit of your womb." come to pass in 1994, but there was also a warning in verse 17. It basically said if the Israelites' hearts turned away and they were not obedient and bowed down to other gods, they would be destroyed. After the first year there were times I had to choose between speaking free at churches or for big money at other places. I hate to admit it, but there were times I would choose the paid speaking engagements over the churches. I started believing my own press and enjoying the prestige that came with the position of head coach too much. Of course, I was not literally bowing down to other gods, but I was prideful and not putting God first.

In 1995, Robert Baldwin and our other key offensive linemen had graduated. Our first game was against Florida State. They offered us a million dollars to play them in Orlando. It was 100 degrees and it wasn't worth it. We should have played them at home. They were trying to position their quarterback for the Heisman trophy and also had Warrick Dunn. They scored over 50 points on us and never took their first team out. The media criticized Bobby Bowden for that, and he called and apologized to me.

The next game was against a good Rutgers team. Our GA, Clay Helton, figured out their signals and we won. It was a big upset. Coach K and his wife Mickie flew with us to the Army game to attend a dinner given in his honor at the West Point Club. He was a West Point graduate and had been Army's basketball coach during the 1970s. Army was motivated to win because in 1994 our young backup quarterback had thrown a touchdown pass on an audible to run up the score, and they hadn't forgotten. The game was a defensive battle. We opened with a touchdown and had a goal line stand the next drive to stop McAda on second and goal at the four. McAda got a concussion and couldn't remember any of his plays. Army's backup quarterback, Thompson, had only thrown one pass in his collegiate career.

The second quarter was a defensive game. Duke led 10-9 at the half. Fischer opened the second half with a 30 yard pass to Marc Wilson. We led 17-9 until Army returned a kickoff 82 yards and scored. They missed a two point conversion and we led 17-15. Duke got a field goal and made it 20-15, but Army answered with a touchdown to make it 21-20 in the third quarter. Duke completed a 39 yard pass on the next series, but it was called back for holding. Army drove to our 34 and missed a field goal, but we couldn't get a drive going and punted with 6:53 left in the fourth quarter. Army stalled and shanked a punt. With 90 seconds left, Fischer threw an eight yard pass to Wilson. He caught it at the 20 and Army's Kotwica knocked the ball loose. Army's cornerback, Muhammad, came up with the fumble. Fortunately for Duke, the referee called it an incomplete pass and gave the ball back to us on third down and nine. Fischer scrambled and made a first at the 19 yard line. Senior Tom Cochran kicked a field goal with eight seconds left to win the game 23-21.

We probably didn't deserve to win that game. They held us to less than 100 rushing yards and a controversial call had kept our last drive alive. I felt like Army had outplayed us, so I went into their locker room after the game and told them they deserved to win. I also apologized for the pass that had run up the score the year before. It didn't make up for a bad call deciding the game, but I wanted them to know I recognized that they fought hard and did everything they could do to win the game.

All of our key defensive figures from the '94 season were injured in the Army game. We went on to lose a close game against Maryland, and blew a nice lead at Virginia to lose that one. We almost beat Carolina, but we were defeated by another big Octavius Barnes play. We finally beat Wake Forest at home and ended the season 3-8. The good team I had inherited graduated when that year ended.

Forced to Retire

I always say I was forced to retire because of illness. They were sick of me. The 1996 season was a disaster. We didn't win a game that year. Because of our injuries, we were playing with 46 freshmen and redshirt freshmen. We looked smaller than a service academy team when we played Army. They were a good bowl team under Bobby Sutton. We lost another tough one when Wake Forest shoved our defensive back out of the way without getting a pass interference call and they won the game. The only positive was that Scottie Montgomery, Ben Ertlejack and a lot of our young players who had no business starting had to start because of injuries and got experience. Scottie remembers making a big mistake in the Northwestern game:

> I was returning a kick and saw a hole on the right side. I was thinking touchdown when a linebacker hit me, and I fumbled. Coach put me back in after I failed and I made All ACC as a returner. Coach Goldsmith believed in me, but he also held me accountable. I felt like football

was the main reason I was at Duke, so I didn't think going to class was any big deal. When Coach found out I skipped, he called my mom at 5:30a.m. She had to be at her job in a textile mill from 6:00a.m.-2:00p.m. before going to her second job. She threatened to skip work and drive to Durham, not even stop the car, and run over me when she found me. Coach Goldsmith knew how to motivate me. He knew how much I respected my mom. I learned I had to work hard to get away with anything, and I could spend less energy doing what I was supposed to be doing. That goes into who I am today as a coach for the Pittsburg Steelers.

That season was the beginning of the end for my career at Duke. The only positive was a goal line stand when we held UNC for four downs at the one yard line. The administration didn't want to roll over my five year contract at the end of the season, but Tom Butters reminded them that I had turned down other offers to talk to big schools two years earlier. He forced the administration to honor my contract and roll it over. Tom was Duke Athletics, and he stood with me just as he had done for Mike Krzyzewski when Duke had demanded that they fire him in his third year.

In 1997 we went 2-9, but at least we broke the losing streak. We were tired of losing to the service academies, so we flew in Chuck Petersen, the offensive coordinator at the USAFA. He showed us how to defend the triple option, and we beat Army and

Navy that year. We finally broke the nation's longest losing streak.

Before the 1998 season I was hopeful that we would be competitive. Spencer Romine was finally coming back, and we had a great running back in Letavious Wilkes. Also, we had just hired Les Koenning, a proven offensive coordinator. While I was on vacation in Franklin, NC that summer, I picked up a football preview magazine and saw that I was named in a "Coaches on the Hot Seat" article.

That was my first inkling that something was amiss. Our old vice chancellor at Duke had stepped down and the new one, Tallman Trask, was making changes and recommendations to the president. When Tom Butters retired for health reasons in 1997, the vice chancellor wanted to bring in the athletic director from Iowa State. I felt like I should support Joe Alleva, who had been the current assistant athletic director at Duke. Vice Chancellor Trask held it against me that I hadn't supported his candidate, even though our Duke president's sister had taught at Iowa State with him and did not recommend him. I probably should have listened to Pam and stayed out of the selection process, but I thought Alleva would protect the football program while Trask was cleaning house and dismissing most of the Duke department heads.

We opened against Western Carolina. We turned the ball over three or four times and saved some of our best plays for the next game but still won 24-7. The next game was against heavily favored

Northwestern. We had lost a heartbreaker to them on fourth and five in 1997, but in 1998 we destroyed them on the road. We scored close to 50 points, which was huge because we recruited against them. I told our sports information director, Mike Cragg, "They won't be able to fire me so quickly now." He said, "There's no way they'll ever fire you." When we flew back into Raleigh Durham International Airport we saw FSU getting on their plane. We knew we were in trouble because NC State had just beaten them and we had to play them the next week.

I had been having stress pains before the Northwestern game, which was normal for me, but they hadn't gone away after the game so I told our trainer, Hap Zarzour, and they did all these stress tests at the Duke Heart Center. I thought I was fine, but the Monday before the FSU game I had to have a heart catheterization. They told me I couldn't do anything strenuous, so I had to watch practice from a golf cart while we got ready for FSU. On Friday we ate boxed lunches from a local restaurant and then did our walk through on the field before flying to Tallahassee. Our FCA share time speaker, Glen Bass, had played against me when he was at ECU and I was at Western Carolina. He was also the pastor at Faith Presbyterian church, the church our family attended when we were at FAMU. Our friends from that church and Rudy Hubbard also came to see us.

Everyone was pumped up for the Saturday pre-game. I was walking around the FSU field when all of a sudden I felt the sickest I have ever felt in my life. I thought something was wrong with my heart and I was going to die right there in Doak Campbell stadium. I had to lie down on the table in the training room for awhile and then sit on the bench on our sidelines. We jumped out to a 10-0 lead. Our kids were saying it was a soft FSU team. By the start of the second quarter, most of the defense felt sick. Richmond Flowers fumbled the kickoff and FSU got a touchdown to get into the game. By halftime we were tied 10-10. The Seminoles had some great receivers that were awfully hard to cover one-on-one, and they won by two or three touchdowns. By the time we got home, almost the whole team was sick. On Monday, 32 players were out sick. Some were in the hospital. We lost our whole defensive front. People were starting to wonder if someone at the hotel had poisoned our food. Then Bowden called and said that his whole offensive line was sick too. Their only offensive player that wasn't sick was their quarterback because we hadn't gotten close to him all day. The doctors determined that it was a contagious virus caused by food poisoning. We guessed it was from the boxed lunches.

Our team couldn't practice that week and it was frustrating because we were good enough to beat Virginia, but they beat us 13-6. We bounced back and beat Clemson to be 4-3 on the last day of October. We had Vanderbilt, Maryland, and UNC coming up. We knew they were all beatable teams and we were feeling good about ourselves. When we started getting ready for Vanderbilt, Romine was injured and Richmond Flowers was out because he had an emergency appendectomy. Before the Vandy game, Alleva told me it was important to win the game. It was important to win every game, so I thought that was strange. Later I found out an alumnus was writing letters to put my job on the line. I saw his cronies at the hotel that night and got suspicious.

We started badly, getting behind a couple of touchdowns at halftime, but were tied in the fourth quarter. Vanderbilt was good that year and they were motivated to keep us out of a bowl. The word was out that if we won six games we would be bowl bound, and Vandy didn't want another academic school to go to a bowl. Late in the fourth, our backup quarterback overthrew a deep ball to Scottie Montgomery. No one had been able to cover Scottie all day. He separated his shoulder diving for the ball, and we had no offense left. Scottie and Richmond were our big guns and we didn't have an offense without them or Romine. We went into double overtime, and Vandy ran a fake field goal to get a key first down in overtime and kicked a field goal to win the game.

We still had all those injuries going into Maryland. They were beatable, and we jumped off to a lead but blew it by throwing several interceptions. Our quarterback was still out, and we got beat by a Maryland team that we could have easily defeated if we had been healthy. Earlier we had lost by one touchdown to NC State. Now I was sitting on the hot seat after losses to Vanderbilt and a bad Maryland team. Johnny Moore worked for the Blue Devil magazine and TV show. He told me there was

something going on with my job, and he had heard
Duke had already contacted Carl Franks. Alleva
wouldn't admit anything. Tom D'Ormi, our assistant
athletic director said, "Fred you'd better win this
game."

Carolina was enjoying the most successful five
years they had ever had. They were really, really good.
UNC had so many players go on to play in the NFL
that year. It was a huge rivalry anyway, but Carolina
had lost the week before so they were even more
motivated to beat us. Our crowd was down for the
game, and that also hurt us. They beat us 21-7.

I met with Joe Alleva in my office the Sunday
after the game, and he told me they were pressuring
him to fire me. He criticized me for not getting rid of a
player who had been in trouble the previous spring, but
Joe had told me himself not to get rid of that player if I
hadn't heard anything from the police. Then he tried to
say my job would have been safe if I had just beaten
Carolina. He didn't fire me then; he said he was going
to think about it and would let me know by the
Wednesday before Thanksgiving. So that Wednesday I
called and couldn't get him. On Thanksgiving, Alleva
told me to come back to Durham to meet with him. I
was waiting on my family to meet me in the mountains
that weekend, so I had to put it off until Monday.

When we met, Alleva asked me if I would like
to resign. I said no. Ken had taught me not to ever
resign. Duke agreed to honor my contract and pay me
for the next four years. I called Pam and said I had

good news and bad news. I had worn a suit to the meeting because I figured I would be doing a press conference one way or the other. I was mistaken. Duke didn't even give me the honor of meeting with the press. A few weeks later Alleva had an assistant call and tell me not to attend the football banquet, so I wasn't able to say goodbye to the players. It was hard, but Duke honored their obligations. They also fired Les Koenning. Then they brought in Carl Franks who had been with Florida, but had never even been a coordinator. Spurrier said he had never called a play in his life. I was criticized for a 17-39 record, but Franks would go 7-45 during his tenure at Duke.

Many fans supported me and wrote letters to the university during the time I was on the hot seat, and I am grateful for their efforts. My teams had never given up. We were rebuilding and getting stronger every year, and our Duke football players were named the College Football Association's Graduation Rate National Champions from 1994-98. Player Mike Hart told me that his father still says, "The worst decision Duke University ever made was to fire Goldsmith."

John Williamson, one of my Arkansas players, just happened to call on the day I was fired by Duke. I hadn't talked to him in years and was surprised to hear from him. John is in ministry now, and he prayed for me on the phone that day. It meant a lot to me to have a former player pray for me in that moment.

Kim Helton offered me a job as an assistant at Houston, but I didn't think Kim was planning on being there longer than a year and I didn't want to go there on a maybe. I was sick of football and I didn't even want to watch the Super Bowl or read the sports section. For the first time in our lives we could live wherever we wanted to live. Pam's parents lived in Franklin so we decided to move there.

The Panther Pit

In 1999 I reconnected with Larry Travis. Larry had helped me get jobs as a graduate assistant at the University of Florida and a coaching job at Gainesville High. In 1999, Larry was the athletic director for Western Carolina. He wanted me to be the assistant AD there and help with fundraising. I was interested, but the chancellor thought I wouldn't stay long. I did end up working for Western broadcasting their football games during the 1999 and 2000 seasons.

In 2001, I heard that Franklin High School was looking for a head football coach. When I heard about it, I remembered a conversation Pam and I had had several years earlier when I was at Duke. We had been on vacation in Franklin, and we were walking around the track at the high school. I told Pam I'd like to coach again for the right reasons and not just to move up to the next level. It was always an ego trip before. I wasn't good enough to play baseball for the Brooklyn Dodgers and, primarily, all my moves were to be at bigger and better schools. I had been raising money to send kids to FCA camp all along, but the next time I wanted it to be more about influencing the players' lives and less about me. In her wisdom Pam said, "Be careful what you wish for; it comes around sometimes."

Franklin High School is in the small town of Franklin, NC. The community revolves around the school and everyone takes high school football seriously. I liked the people, and I really thought long and hard about whether to apply for the job at Franklin High School because this was the hometown we wanted to settle down in, and I didn't want to disappoint the people. I met Franklin's principal, Gary Shields, at a football game. I used to go to all the games with my golfing buddies, Grady Corbin, Pete Penland, Norman Seay, and Vic Teague. Mr. Shields and I had the same goals for the football program. He said:

> I learned early that academics and sports had to maintain a balance, but a winning athletic program and a band were two visuals that the public used to evaluate the success or failure of a school. Also, these two programs identify your school locally, regionally, and within the state. Pride in one's school is of the utmost importance because pride transfers into positive self-esteem, better academics, and fewer dropouts.

FHS had community support and an active booster club that had raised money for a 6,000 square foot football facility. They also had adopted a "Bigger, Faster, Stronger" motto for their weight conditioning program and had experienced success in the 1990s when Shawn Bryson and Sandy Tabor had gotten college scholarships. Josh and Jay Brooks had returned to FHS to coach after playing college football in the late 90s. FHS was on college recruiters' radar and Shields wanted to make sure it stayed there. He said:

> We needed a leader and experienced coach. He had to assist the principal in leading the school, community, and athletic department into believing that the twenty first century was a new era. Fred took on the challenge and within five years his record was 47-14. Looking back over my 21 years as principal, the saying "surrounding yourself with good people will make you look good" could never have been more true. Leadership was a unique quality Coach Goldsmith had not only on campus, but also in the community.

I prayed about the job and told Kevin Corbin, the chairman of the school board, "I think I know where you can get a good coach." He said, "Who?" I said, "Me." My wife's cousin Pete, a diehard FHS fan, cautioned, "Only take it if you and the players can have fun again." I tried to make it fun and loosened up by scheduling practices when it was cooler. It was the first time I was completely motivated to be a witness for the Lord with those kids. I had come full circle from where I could have been after our Cinderella season at Duke when Pam and I walked the FHS track. That year I had been the Bobby Dodd Coach of the

Year, and I had turned down interviews at LSU and Oklahoma.

When I took the job, I also became the civics teacher. I had to get recertified because the state of Florida had destroyed my NTE scores so there was no proof that I had passed the test, even though I had a Florida teaching certificate. I knew I had gotten a good score, but there was no proof. I took the PRAXIS and wrote a note on my test that I was 57 years old and knew the stuff but had never written a lesson plan in my life. I left the last 10 questions blank and was worried that I hadn't passed. I even sent in a check to take it again. I wound up passing the lesson plan part and getting a new teaching certificate. I enjoyed teaching history and being a part of the faculty. Mr. Shields said:

> His age and life experience allowed him to see history made and allowed him to share experiences and testimony that supported the textbook. What set Coach Goldsmith apart from other coaches is that he was not just a single minded football coach. He loved and supported all the student athletes, even from other schools in the conference. He may not have known it, but his recommendation was the only one a recruiter needed. He willingly shared his student athletes with other sports and attended their other events.

After I took the job in the spring of 2001, reality hit. It was humbling to have to fix urinals and stock toilet paper in the locker room. I realized there was a big difference between being a Division I head football coach and a high school head football coach. 21 of the 22 starters from the previous season had graduated, and it had been 20 years since Franklin had had a winning season. We had always been kind of a country club school. Basketball, tennis, and golf were bigger than football, but we had potential. Dustin Penland and Josh Durm were good players on our JV team. We also had tremendous fan support. When we had our first scrimmage against Swain County, everyone was revved up and the atmosphere felt like Texas high school football.

We lost our first home game against a great Murphy team by one, 14-13, when we hooked a field goal attempt. After the frustration at the end of the game, I realized the team and the staff had a lot of growing up to do. My golfing buddy, Norman Seay, came down to the dressing room after the game to console and encourage me. After that we went on to have a fantastic 10-2 season. Reflecting on those early years at FHS, Josh Brooks said:

I will always be indebted to Coach Goldsmith because he gave me a tremendous opportunity with a lot of responsibility at an early age in my coaching career. He allowed me a chance to make some tough decisions while I knew he would back me 100%. He mentored me and my twin brother when he didn't have to. He put up with our immaturity, pouting, and opinionated attitudes, all the while teaching us every aspect of the game of football. I thank God he didn't quit on us, and I look back at how much I have learned from him as a coach, deacon of the church, a man of God, a leader of his family, and someone who stands up for what he believes in. I am truly a much better person, teacher, father, and coach today because of the impact Coach Goldsmith had on my life. It is an honor to call him my friend, and the only thing I hate is the fact that I never had a chance to play for him myself. Coach was given a platform many years ago and he has used every bit of it to make a positive difference in the lives of those that have been lucky enough to know him.

The next game was a hot, muggy night and we were 40 points ahead of Rabun County when we pulled our starters out at halftime. We were winning, but we weren't getting along as well as we could have as a team. Our captains told me to kick Brandon Penland off the team. I told them them was related to my wife, and I couldn't kick a Penland off the team. Even though we had a great win, it was followed by a sad week. The day after the game, Pam came into the coaches' office to tell me Norman had died of a heart attack. We buried Norman on that unforgettable Tuesday, September 11, 2001.

We were the underdogs in the Enka game. Before the game, their coach said we were like they had been the year before. He told me next year might be our year. We wound up winning by a couple of touchdowns and knew we might have a chance to be pretty good.

Irwin was the co-favorite with Enka, loaded with talent, and they had won big the week before. I told the team, "We won't put on pads all week long. We need to have more energy than they do; we'll practice in shorts, you go to bed early all week; we'll get in a dogfight." We went into overtime and went up by three with a Garner field goal and our defensive tackle, Adam Garrett, made an interception to win the game. Their coach, Travis Nolan, had played quarterback for Jerry Moore at Appalachian. We prayed with Travis and his wife after the game.

We beat Tuscola next, and I got a 15 yard penalty that wasn't my fault. There was a sports editor dressed in a coaching shirt yelling at the officials from the sidelines, and they mistook him for me. Later on it was a thrill to beat our big rival, Smoky Mountain, 47-15. The game was also memorable because Smoky Mountain's mascot was a horse that got out of control and went running around the field. I dove out of the way, but he knocked Coach Plemmons down. Needless to say, after a complaint by our principal, that was the last time Smoky Mountain brought a horse to our football field.

The next week we had an open date. I was shocked to hear that Smoky Mountain beat TC Roberson. TC had been undefeated in the conference and was tied with us for first place. Mike Houston, TC Roberson's coach at that time, is from Franklin, and I am sure he had been looking forward to playing us for the championship.

Our last game of the season, we played TC at home. Everyone was fired up. The lights went out and the game was delayed 45 minutes. Their quarterback was hurt and we jumped out ahead. We thought it would be easy, but we battled back and forth until finally their best players gave out while we two platooned our players, except for Josh Durm who had to play tailback and safety. We outlasted them that day, won the Mountain Athletic Conference championship and hosted the first playoff game. We were eliminated in the second round, but we tied the school record for the deepest playoff run in 29 years.

I was fortunate enough to be voted the Western NC Coach of the Year by the *Asheville Citizen Times*. My friend Dr. Danny Lotz told me that he and his wife Anne had been visiting his father-in-law, Dr. Billy Graham, on Christmas morning. According to Danny, the award was mentioned in the newspaper that day and Dr. Graham read about it and said he was glad that I had won the championship because I was a Christian coach. That meant so much to me because I had accepted Christ through his preaching ministry. That was a glorious first year at Franklin, and it was similar to our first year at Duke when we were blessed with many wins and didn't have any injuries.

After that first season, we realized we didn't have enough seats to host the crowds at the playoff games. We worked with our boosters to get community leaders involved in renovating our stadium. We called the renovation the CBS project. That stood for concessions, bathrooms, and seating. Ronnie Beale spearheaded the effort. The community provided over $250,000 in cash and in-kind gifts.

We were excited going into the 2002 season and had most of the boys and the entire coaching staff back. Jay and Josh Brooks were back coaching the offense, Bobby Kuppers coached the secondary, Billy Crane coached the outside linebackers, Tony Plemmons coached the defensive line, and I coached linebackers and running backs. Chris and Josh Durm were back. Josh Durm would rush for around 1,800 yards and win an award for the best football player in Western NC at the end of the year. Our experienced quarterback, Clay Wyatt, threw 31 touchdown passes and only had four interceptions. I told the coaches we needed to start praying for an underclass backup quarterback for Clay, and a couple of days later a new quarterback and linebacker, Cecil Pollock, moved in from Georgia.

A USA Today reporter shadowed us the week we beat Irwin, and he wrote a great story. We had some easy victories early on against Murphy and Enka. Our only loss of the regular season came against Asheville High and cost us the conference championship. It was pouring down rain and we blew a 10 point lead by making some mistakes in the third quarter. First our punter dropped a wet ball; then on third and 10, we got a 15 yard penalty for roughing the passer. The referee who called it was the same guy who called a penalty on Chris Combs for saluting the Virginia bench at the Duke Virginia game in 1998. Asheville scored, but we were still up by three. Then we bounced a pass off our receiver's hands with three minutes to go, and Asheville picked it off to set up their winning score. We didn't have any other close games.

We beat Smoky Mountain in the playoffs with some defense I had used at Arkansas. We blitzed and sacked the quarterback 11 times. We beat a very good TC team again to advance to the playoffs. We won the first round of the playoffs, then met an excellent South Point team in round two; I have never been so cold in a game. It was 25 degrees with the wind blowing hard. We went back and forth. Chris Durm made a long run down to the 11, and then we threw a counter bootleg pass behind our All State receiver, Dustin Penland. They intercepted it, or we would have been up by three scores and that would have been the game. Instead, we got tired and lost by a touchdown. That was the best high school game I have ever seen. I still look back and wonder if I could have done a better job stopping the flexbone. That year South Point went to the state finals, and the next year they won the state championship. We went 11-2 and tied the school record for victories.

In 2003, we lost a lot of good players from our 2002 team. Cayman Brooks, Chris Durm and Cecil Pollock were back. Cecil had been our starting linebacker in 2002, and in 2003 he had to assume the role of starting quarterback as well. In our opening game we went to Hayesville and led most of the first half until they went up by a touchdown with a Hail Mary. We took a lightning break, and I was ready to call it off. The other coach, Neil Setzer, had five guys in the locker room with cramps, so neither of us wanted to finish. We had a choice of having it as a game that didn't count, so we wound up with 10 countable games.

We threw an interception on the first play of the Murphy game, and they ran it back for a touchdown, but we finally won the game by a couple of touchdowns.

We had a good season for a rebuilding year. Our last two games were a great climax to the regular season. We went to Smoky Mountain for the next to last regular season game. Smoky's coach, Tim Hawkins, brought back their legendary coach, Babe Howell, to give the pregame speech. They were all pumped up to beat us because we were their big rival. With the score tied 7-7, Cayman Brooks blocked a field goal, then we went on a long drive highlighted by a Cecil Pollock play action pass to Eric Prevett for a key first down, some tough running by Chris Durm, and Cecil scoring on fourth and four with a an option keep. We sacked their quarterback late and ended the game with a 14-7 victory. Every time we beat Smoky, I celebrated by taking the players to Ryan's Steakhouse and buying them all the steak they could eat. Chris Durm ate seven steaks that night!

TC Roberson was the last game. They were better than us, but Josh Brooks came up with a strategy to hold the ball. He was an old school coach like his dad and me, so I liked the idea. We used most of the clock every play and kept the ball. We got into a big battle and it was 7-7 pretty late in the fourth quarter when we ran a swing screen 45 yards to Prevett to set up the winning touchdown, a score made possible by tough runs by Chris and Cecil. They came back and we stopped them on fourth and one.

We lost to Asheville and Tuscola in close games. East Henderson had a great running back that rushed for 200 yards, but we still beat them by 20 points. We went back to the playoffs and destroyed our first round opponent at home, but we had to go back to South Point for the second playoff game. We didn't roll our safety over like we should have to defend the triple option. They beat us by about four touchdowns and went on to win State. I didn't feel bad because we were 8-3 and it was supposed to be a down year.

Matt Corbin made his first field goal in 2003. Matt started out as a soccer player and ended up playing for me for six years, both at Franklin High School and at Lenior Rhyne University. Matt is now in dental school at UNC and wanted to share some of his own stories:

> It was time for the first Thursday walkthrough of the season. I had never done this before, but I had watched a Thursday practice before and all I remember is that you actually *walk through* the different plays to fine tune everyone for the Friday night contest. The ball wasn't run at full speed, the receivers weren't running routes, and the ball wasn't thrown

much, if at all…*merely a walk through*. After warm ups and stretching, and maybe a few offensive plays, Coach G called for the field goal unit: He screamed, 'FIELD GOAL! FIELD GOAL! FIELD GOAL!' I get out there, line up for the kick, and before I can *walk through* my responsibilities, I hear, 'Corbin, where is your kicking block?' (In the high school game you can "tee up" a field goal by using a one or two inch block… I used a one inch block to Coach G's dismay, but that's another story). We had a series of exchanges in which I tried to explain I figured I needn't bring my block since this was, in fact, a *walk through*. He wasn't impressed with my rationale or with me stalling practice. He, as politely as a head coach can be to a kicker, told me to RUN and get that darn block. The field house happened to be at the other end of the field! As I was running to get the block, and digging frantically through my bag of football gear, and running back…he was fervently *educating* the team on the importance of preparedness. As I was on my way back, the *education* switched from a team focus back to me. As I placed the block in the appropriate position next to my holder, Preston Sanders, I was still getting *educated*. As I lined up to kick, I'm still getting *educated*. As the ball is being snapped, and I approach the ball…yep still getting that *education*. Finally, contact is made, the balls rises and sails through the uprights. Coach looks at me, smiles, and says, 'Great kick, Corbin.' The team got an education at my expense and I never forgot that three inch by three inch piece of hard black rubber again.

Coach and I had become close during my high school days. We both shared a love of our families, our hometown, our church, and our Lord. We were both members of Holly Springs Baptist Church in Franklin, NC. After a Sunday morning church service, coach asked me if I ever wanted to quit playing *that communist sport* and join the football team as a kicker. I fell in love with the game. I played both soccer and football that season, but gave up the roundball in order to focus on my kicking game the next year. Coach had just installed some narrowed field goal posts and expressed a lot of faith in me as his upcoming kicker. Had he not asked me to give football a try, I never would have played under the lights in a small mountain town that virtually shuts down for Friday night games at The Pit. I would never have had the opportunity to beat Smoky Mountain by a field goal my senior year and share the Player of the Game honors with my pal, Preston Sanders. I would have never made the decision to play collegiate ball and have my college education nearly paid for, and I would have never met my beautiful wife, Charissa. I am forever thankful for those opportunities and my time under the ole ball coach and for the success and leadership he brought to the communities in and around Franklin and Hickory, NC. He taught us a lot about football, but taught us more about life. He also, when appropriate, related the game to our walk with Christ and taught us how to *act like somebody*. I have no reservation when I say that Coach G., the stellar staff he put together, and the guest speakers he brought to our team helped mold me into the man I am today.

In 2004 we had lost Chris Durm, Cayman Brooks, and Cecil Pollock to graduation. We had ninth and tenth graders playing linebacker and a new safety, Daniel Gibbs. It was hard to replace Durm, and we didn't have size or age on our defensive front. 2004 was also the year that Hurricane Ivan interrupted our Asheville High game. We had changed the game to Thursday to beat the storm. It stopped raining during the pregame warm up in Asheville and didn't look that bad. Asheville had two players who went to the NFL later, Johnny White, who played for the Buffalo Bills, and Cresden Butler, who played for the Pittsburgh Steelers. They were good and they were leading us 17-0 at the half.

On the advice of the Asheville Police Department, we called the game at the half because Hurricane Ivan had moved into western NC much faster than had been anticipated. We had to take detours back to Macon County. Franklin fire trucks met us as we came into town; the firemen said the roads had gone from bad to worse. When we got back to the school, we had to pump water out of our flooded equipment room. All the players were supposed to call when they got home, and two guys didn't call until 1:30a.m. Our phone had stayed on until then, and as soon as the last boy was accounted for, it went out. I got some flak for taking them to Asheville and should have listened when Jewel Drake told us not to go to the game. That Thursday night was the night houses slid off the mountain on Peek's Creek. It was a horrible tragedy for the community and put winning and losing in perspective.

Early in the season we had beaten Rabun County and Murphy, but we couldn't beat Robbinsville. They were a I A team with five seniors out, and their best player was injured in the second quarter. We dropped a Hail Mary pass on the last play in the end zone, but that was OK because they were well coached and deserved to win. We struggled through that year and got demolished by undefeated TC Roberson, 47-7. We pulled a huge upset against Tuscola. They had the best quarterback in the league. Jonathan Crompton was highly recruited. He started for four years at Tennessee and went to the NFL. I knew if we could run the ball we could control the clock. Late in the fourth quarter when we were trying to run the clock down, we handed the ball to Alex Croteau, who went 65 yards for a touchdown. This gave Tuscola and Crompton time to drive and score. They attempted an onsides kick. It was fielded by our toughest guy, Daniel Gibbs, who got three onsides kicks that night. We took a knee and a pulled a huge upset, ending the regular season 6-5.

In the playoffs we had to play South Point, the defending state champions, for the third straight year. It had poured two days and the field was all thick mud. I used Monty Kiffen's system for defending the triple option and put in the final touches on taking away the passing game against the slot receivers. They couldn't get anything going between the mud and the strategy. We beat them by a couple of touchdowns and they only gained one yard rushing. Our 2004 and 2005 starting quarterback, Chase Holland, threw a perfect pass from our own one yard line and we won the game, even with our all time leading rusher benched for disciplinary reasons. We ended our playoff run with another loss against Winston Salem Carver; we just couldn't run with them. We were inept at tackling and got beat 41-25. After the season, I told my principal and athletic director I was about ready to retire. Mr. Shields asked me to think it over and wait until after the holidays to decide.

I decided to coach another year. I could tell that the next team was going to be special from the way they trained hard in the offseason. I wasn't sure if we would have our star running back, though. He got in big trouble in January, so I made him do a weekly Bible study with me and told him he had to stay out of trouble until August. He complied and broke all the school's rushing records and got a college scholarship offer. Our team had experience and confidence. As a result, our only close game was a 33-31 upset of TC

Roberson at home. Expectations were running high in 2005. Gary Shields recalls:

> The night we played Asheville, we had standing room only 45 minutes before kickoff. Coach Goldsmith in his wisdom looked at me and said, 'We may have created a monster.' I have since thought about how much stress coaches feel and what is expected by the community. One losing season and a coach can go from hero to goat.

When we played Asheville High we were 10-0 and both teams were undefeated. People were in their seats three hours before the game. Asheville said they had never played in that atmosphere. We lost by a touchdown, but they were a great team. Our defensive backs were small and couldn't stop Johnny White's size and 4.4 speed. We dominated everyone else and won the first and second rounds of the playoffs. We almost beat TW Andrews in the third round. We thought we had the winning touchdown when Preston Sanders made a great catch in the end zone. We just couldn't stop them and they scored as the clock was running out. TW Andrews went on to play Asheville in the state championship game. It was a great, great year for our quarterback, Chase Holland, and our receiver, Preston Sanders. They broke every receiving and passing record that year. We finished 12-2. I thought it was a good time to step down.

Even though I had determined to coach for the right reasons at Franklin High School, my priorities started changing. I cared about winning too much. I am ashamed to admit it, but that last year I made some stupid mistakes. Pam was in a car wreck near the school, and when she said she was fine I stayed in a meeting with the players instead of checking on her. I also asked a player's dad if he really needed to miss a game to go to his grandma's funeral.

At the end of the season, my overall record from 2001-2005 was 47-15, and I held the record for the most wins in Franklin football history. It didn't pay like Duke, but I wouldn't trade those five years for anything; they were my happiest in 45 years of coaching. Since then, my former offensive coordinator, Josh Brooks, has had a successful tenure as the FHS head coach and broken my record for the most games won at Franklin High School

In 2006, I retired from football and enjoyed attending the Franklin games as a fan. When Josh's unbeaten team faced an undefeated Asheville team, Congressional candidate Heath Shuler sat with Pam und me at the game. We knew him because he had helped FCA by buying Bibles. He was probably one of the few Democrats Pam ever voted for. He won the election and has led weekly Congressional Bible studies ever since. Franklin was the better team, but they dropped a late pass and lost the game. The Panthers won 12 games that year, and have continued to win. They won 13 straight games in 2011. Today I watch the FHS games with great pride in the team and Josh's coaching staff.

Lenoir Rhyne Returns to Glory

After my second retirement from football, I was enjoying working with the FCA coaches' ministry because I got to speak to teams and work with coaches all over western North Carolina. One of my speaking engagements was for the Lenoir Rhyne football team, and I knew their FCA director, David Daly. I had been approached by their athletic director, Neill McGeachy, about coaching at LR in 2001 and he brought it back up in 2007.

Neill is a salesman, and it was easy for him to play on my ego. He worked on me for a couple of weeks. First, he asked me to play in a golf tournament in Hickory with some of the LR alumni, Hank McCrory and Bob Miller. I won a Hooters golf bag that day and traded it in for some sunglasses. Then he asked for a recommendation from Tom Butters since Tom had been my athletic director at Duke and Neill had been the Duke basketball coach before Coach K. Tom told him I was the best coach he had ever hired, including Coach K, but that was a stretch. When Neill called and said they were making a change in the football program, I wasn't interested because I knew the situation hadn't been good for the staff when I had checked into the job in 2001. The pay was terrible; they would have to add salaries for two more coaches to be competitive. Pam thought I ought to talk to him. I think she was already getting tired of me being retired. Before I made any plans, I had to think about what I would be giving up. I enjoyed my friends in Franklin and the FCA ministry. I also had to see if Lenoir Rhyne could be competitive since I knew the disadvantages of being at an academic school after my experiences with Rice and Duke.

The negotiations began, and we went back and forth. Neill asked me what I thought a decent salary would be. I told him I wanted to be paid as much as the highest paid coach in the league. He agreed to that, but the money wasn't as important as the ability to recruit and be successful. Next, I met with Rachel Nichols, the admissions director. She convinced me that we could make it work and agreed to let football players in with the NCAA minimum requirements. I had never had that advantage with Rice in the SWC or Duke in the ACC, and thought we would be on equal footing with the other teams in the South Atlantic Conference. I didn't realize at the time how rigorous the academics were or how hard it would be for players to stay in school. Recruiting is a whole different ballgame in Division II. Nobody gets a full ride for sports. Coaches have to work with financial aid for need based and academic scholarships and piecemeal it all together, so the admissions director plays a huge role in recruiting.

The next challenge would be hiring coaches. The salaries for the assistant coaches were lower than what most high school coaches were making. First, I called Roger Hinshaw because I had worked with him at the AFA and Arkansas. After years of coaching college ball, he was coaching high school in Houston; he thought he could come. Then I hired Blake Harrell, a hardworking young coach from Franklin. His wife Deonna was a great coach's wife, and I knew she would be an asset as well. Then Roger backed out, so I interviewed Mike Houston from TC Roberson for the defensive coordinator position. He was from Franklin and had a year of college experience at Brevard College under his belt. I met with the rest of the remaining LR staff and decided to keep them because we couldn't match the Franklin High School salaries to bring any more of my former staff. Brian Hill turned out to be a good defensive line coach from the original LR staff. Ron Boyd, our offensive line coach, was a fast learner and he got better and better. Kyle Garner, my kicker from Franklin, came on as a graduate assistant.

The first year was rough. In 2007 we were basically starting from scratch with a bad team. We were young, inexperienced, slow on defense, and out of shape. Our first game was against VA Union, and our first team quarterback, Justin Sanders, got hurt right away and missed most of the season with a broken hand. We had to put in a true freshman quarterback who started all year and struggled.

Then we played Appalachian the week after they beat Michigan. I knew we were in trouble, but I also knew that Jerry Moore would hold the score down because we were good friends. A transfer from Appalachian who had also played for me at Franklin, Preston Sanders, set up our only score. The final result was 48-7. I was happy to get out of there without any more injuries.

We started to see a little improvement in the Davidson game. Andrew Courman had a great day that day. We came back and took the lead late in the fourth quarter. The whole second half we played great. We had a strong safety injured and the backup sprained his ankle in the pregame warm-up so we had to play a true freshman, Marcus Shuford. He got beat on a play and they took the lead, but we were driving down in field goal range and made a first down with 37 seconds to go. After our receiver made the catch in field goal range, he had the first and was tackled and stripped of the ball. I was feeling sick after that game as much as almost any game except the 1987 Arkansas-Texas game. It would get better, though. Marcus would go on to be a team captain and become the defensive player of the year for the SAC his senior year.

We went on to win against Benedict College. The Brevard game was embarrassingly close because they had just started a football program the year before. They had Josh Durm from Franklin and I had his brother Chris. Chris ran over Josh, and we scored and picked up a fumble for a late touchdown and the win. We only won two games that first year.

In 2008, we still were a young, inexperienced team, but the atmosphere was slowly changing. The alumni saw a difference when our players showed up in the sports section for football instead of off campus incidents. We brought Tommy Laurendine as offensive coordinator to run the triple option, hired Brian Rucker to coach receivers, and moved Kyle Garner to running backs.

We lost a heartbreaker to Mars Hill after blowing a 10 point halftime lead. Corbin shanked his first two punts with the wind at his back and we fumbled deep in our territory at the beginning of the second half. Corbin was frustrated:

> Coach would light into me each time I came off the field. Sure the yelling was expected at first, but the way our team was playing on both sides of the ball had him livid. He knew we were better and more prepared than what the scoreboard showed, and he had seen enough mistakes to last the rest of the season. The repetitive berating was well-deserved, but it wasn't helping the punting unit and it sure as heck wasn't helping my punting. I wanted to defend our punt unit, but it didn't matter… we had a job to do and we weren't doing it. On the fourth or fifth punt of the day, he lit into us again and at me specifically. I finally stopped holding back my emotions and told him sternly, 'If you'd quit yelling at me, maybe I'd punt better.' He told me, 'If you punt better, maybe I'll quit yelling!'

The coaches were getting impatient and questioning the systems. It was one of the hardest tests of leadership that I have had. I explained we had to develop the players and it would take some time for them to grow up. It turned out down the road that some of those same kids made All Conference. At the end of the year we lost two coaches. Between them they had been making about $65,000. I interviewed John Scott from Western Carolina University and he would have been great, but our president put a freeze on hiring. I had to go all spring without two coaches, and then LR took $40,000 from our salaries and used the money to start a lacrosse program. I felt like we were being punished for only winning three games because I had been a Division I coach and was expected to turn it around quicker. They may have wanted me to quit, but they weren't going to fire me because they didn't have the money to pay me off.

I could see we were getting better running the triple option. I knew we had to improve defensively. I went to a clinic and learned that Vandy had just won a bowl game with the zone blitz defense, so we decided to use that with our team. I also felt like the big play in college football was the zone read option out of the shotgun; Dinger had used that at Rice with Bert Emanuel. I knew there had to be a better way to defend that. Joe Paterno's book, *Football My Way*, explained a defense he had used to save his job in 1968, and I used that philosophy to change our defense. We decided to stop the run and make them pass. We didn't have time to practice defending against the zone like we had at

Air Force, so we practiced the zone blitzing because we didn't have the personnel we had had at Arkansas or Rice to be able to defend against four or five receivers.

We tried to disguise what zone we were in, and it worked in 2009. We jumped up to five wins. We beat our biggest rival, Catawba, dominated Davidson 42-0, and had a big upset over Tusculum. The rest were close losses that we lost by a total of 17 points. We had never played Carson Newman close, but we stuck it out and they didn't beat us until our 5'8" second team corner got beat by their receiver at the end of the game. Wingate blocked a field goal that would have won the game for us and beat us 50-49. Concord was another close game; we had gone ahead with 90 seconds left and couldn't get a first. They kicked a 40 yard field goal to tie on the last play of the game, and we lost in overtime. We held Newberry until they broke out for a touchdown at the end of the game. That was typical of all our close games that year. Mars Hill was the only game we didn't play well in. They beat us 24-7.

I was pleased with the way the program was turning around. Our defense was getting better, and the players were stepping up and maturing. We also had one of the top three Division II rushing offenses in the nation. All of a sudden LR began to believe and it all solidified. I hired Joel Taylor from South Carolina State to help Mike Houston with the secondary, and Roy Tesh from Brevard took the defensive line job. The kids really connected with Roy, and he got an intense effort out of our defense. Laurendine went to the Citadel and we replaced him with Brent Thompson from Bucknell. He became our offensive coordinator, quarterback, and fullback coach. Thompson was a wishbone whiz. He was decisive and the kids looked up to him. We hired his wife as a trainer and she made a tremendous contribution as well. Chris Coleman from NC State came to coach the receivers. We were able to replace coaches who left with high quality coaches, and we put in a new punting system from Wofford. There was a renewed effort in everything we did from the kicking game to each position. We should have had a winning season in that third year, but even finishing 5-6, the players and coaches were starting to believe we would win.

After the first year, I realized that there were no easy majors at Lenoir Rhyne. We had the toughest academics in the conference, so we decided to recruit better students. As a result, we had fewer discipline problems and smarter kids who were able to handle the academics and earn the respect of the faculty. Mentally, spiritually, and physically, everything was on the upswing going into that fourth year.

Dal Shealy, former FCA president, recalls:

> Fred was the catalyst by which God moved and worked to help my son Lance build the foundation for FCA in Hickory and the 11 county area. He left programs better than he found them whether as a volunteer with FCA or as a coach. At LR, he recruited character

coaches and players and built the program on Christian principles. The FCA leaders had been praying for access to the football program. Almost immediately, Goldsmith was hired and told David Daly, 'I want you here as much as you can be here.' Daly was instrumental in helping FCA acquire a house on campus for students in leadership. It housed a dozen or so athletes; several were football players. Supporters donated video games and a ping pong table. This house became a good alternative to a fraternity and offered a center for Christian activities on campus.

Huddle groups were promoted at practice, LR started having pregame share time speakers, and players who were in FCA leadership began leading the team and their opponents in prayer after the games. At that point in his career, faith was more important to Fred than football.

We got David an office on campus so he could spend more time with the kids and coaches. It was rewarding to see changed lives during the time I was at LR. The FCA program grew larger and the players were making a difference on campus. Chandler Rearden had been influenced by his high school coach and had come in as a Christian and relaxed his standards as first, but he came back around; he and Major Heron were strong witnesses for Christ. Three guys came to Chandler's room one night just because they saw a difference in his life, and he was able to lead them to the Lord. In addition to supporting FCA, our staff noticed that many of the players came from single parent homes, so we tried to have the coaches' wives around the team to model healthy marriages.

Daly remembers:

> Fred turned the campus around for Christ. When I first came, LR players were an embarrassment to the community. Some of them left when he brought discipline to the program. Coaches and players cleaned up their language, and players who had been troublemakers became team leaders. They never doubted that he loved and cared for them. He became a surrogate dad to many of them. His players could see how to walk the Christian life, and his coaches could see how a Christian marriage worked. Fred made sure his walk matched his talk the whole time he was there.

> 2010 began with an easy first win. We struggled against Concord in the second game. We got a bad call for illegal use of hands inside their 10 when we were driving to win the game. It put us outside the 30, so we missed a 46 yard field goal on the last play. We got another big win at Davidson and Tusculum. With five wins under our belt, we had three tough games left. We lost our homecoming game to Mars Hill after losing a 17-3 lead. We fumbled a kick and still had a chance. We held them at their 30 on third and five, but we got called for a facemask, and they went on to score a shocking 50 yard touchdown run with no time left in the game. We went to Wingate as

the better team, but got beat by one point. The year before we had blown a big 42-21 win at home against them. We blew another lead and lost the chance to win the championship.

We had not beaten Carson Newman in 32 years, but we found a new way to play the option. The first weekend in November it was snowing like crazy in Tennessee all the way through the second quarter of our game. They scored first, then we scored fast on a long pass from all conference quarterback Major Heron to all conference receiver Nick Stutts. Next we went up 14-7 but fumbled around our own 25. After that, we were hot and won 52-14. It could have been worse than that. I remember asking Daly if I should call off the dogs midway through the third quarter. David said, "Don't you dare after what they did to you two years ago, let them enjoy it." David Daly made a tremendous contribution to our program and he was literally by my side throughout all my years at LR, sitting beside me on every bus ride. He had been with me two years earlier when we had been beaten so badly at Carson Newman, so when we won, it was a great experience to have him share that with me. Carson Newman gave us our sixth win and we broke the 32 year losing streak.

The Bears had come full circle. In 2007 Carson Newman had beaten us 45-7. When our teams prayed together at midfield after the game that year, I told both squads and the Carson Newman head coach, my dear friend Ken Sparks, that our goal was to achieve their level. Earlier that year, Neill told me we would never be as good as Carson Newman, but to please one day, be better for three hours. I am thrilled that for two years (2010 and 2011) all our dreams came true for the LR Bears.

Grant Teaff and Dal Shealy were in the press box to see it. I had played against Grant's Baylor teams when we were at Arkansas and Rice, and Grant and I have been friends for many years. I learned so much about coaching and being a Christian from him. When I was a young coach in 1975, I noticed that Grant brought his wife to the coaching convention. I was impressed by that, and I vowed then that if I ever became a head coach, I would follow his example and bring Pam with me. When I first became the head coach at Rice, Grant was a mentor who took me under his wing and told me how he had rebuilt the Baylor program. His wife Donell had welcomed Pam and involved her in the coaches' wives activities when we were in the Southwest Conference together. I was honored when he presented me with the FCA Grant Teaff Lifetime Achievement Award in 2011.

We ended our season with a 7-4 win at home against our biggest rival, Catawba. Major Heron was our quarterback and he had the bull by the horns. Our offensive line was doing well, the backs, Courman and Pone were doing well, and Brandon Martin led the league in sacks to make All-Conference. We also had Nick Stutts, a former walk on quarterback who wasn't fast but worked hard and ran a 4.6 and became the leading receiver in the league. The same kids the coaches had been whining about two years earlier had matured. Chandler Reardon had made all American in 2010, he was coming back, and we led the nation in rushing for Division II.

Matt Corbin stuck it out with me in football and ran track as well. He set the school record in the 800 meter race at the 2010 Lenoir Rhyne Invitational. He says:

> As I completed my first lap and entered the curve in fourth place, there were hundreds of people yelling and cheering. Oh, but I heard only one. There he was, cheering me on, with 300 meters to go. I ended up finishing first. There was something about his voice that made me run faster… maybe I had thought I forgot my kicking block again.

It was so satisfying to build that program back. No one really had an understanding about what it was like when football had been treated differently in the old days. Before the season, I had read *Ten Men You Meet in the Huddle* by Bill Curry. It explained what a rite of passage it was in the 1960s to play football when football was King in the South. At Lenoir Rhyne, they had been treating football like any other sport, and they didn't understand what it would mean to have a good football program that filled the stadium and what that could bring to the campus. We delivered that kind of program and set the wheels in motion for people to see what it was like to have a winning team. I made up my mind to retire after recruiting and spring practice. I wanted Mike Houston to replace me.

It was hard to leave our good friends in our church and neighborhood in Hickory, and it was hard to leave the players and our FCA staff, but I knew it was the right time to leave when Ronnie Beal and I walked off the field after the Carson Newman game. He said, "It'll never get any better than this; it's time to go home." I have no regrets about leaving football when I did. In 2011, Houston and Lenior Rhyne beat Catawba to win the school's first SAC Championship since 1994. I loved watching them win and hearing that there was standing room only at their football banquet.

Because I was retired, I was able to return to Duke in September to see many of my former players and celebrate the hundredth anniversary of Duke football. We live about two hours away from all our grandchildren and I have more time to spend with family and friends. I enjoy working with the FCA coaches' ministry, working with Area Director Rod Brandt and my colleague Dolphus Brown, and visiting western NC high school coaches and huddle leaders. It also has been rewarding to reconnect with Western Carolina football and their fine staff led by Coach Mark Speir.

Monday Morning Quarterback

It is much easier to look back after time and make decisions. Having time to reflect, I am looking back at what I've learned about God, life, coaching, and what a second time around might be like. At 68, I feel life revolves around a walk with or without God, and being in tune with him has a positive effect on our relationships with people and family. I can really see that when I take the time to make pleasing the Lord a habit and pray about all things, there is a peace about relationships, decisions, triumphs, and adversities.

Unfortunately, I know in spite of being a believer, for too long I left God in a corner of life. He was to be called on only at times I couldn't handle circumstances myself and to be worshipped at my convenience at church or FCA meetings. God wants to be there for our decisions, needs, celebrations and comfort. Revelation 3:20 says, "He knocks on the door." It is talking about the door of our hearts. If I had opened that door more, I know I could have "walked the walk "more and "talked the talk" less.

Looking back as a coach and dealing with people makes me wish that I had prayed about every decision. I would have prayed about game strategies before staff meetings rather than just at crucial times on Friday night and Saturday afternoon. Most of all, I would have liked to have stayed in constant prayer and in step with God in dealing with people at home or work. Believe me, most of my problems came from forging ahead without humbly seeking God's wisdom first. For instance, life is too short to hurt others. Praying will bring God into our circumstances and allow us to treat others in a way that pleases Him rather than our egos. Just imagine praying for His direction about every job, every person hired, and every player recruited. Not only that, but what would happen if we prayed every time we spoke to someone? I know that when I did do it His way there was always a peace. I am ashamed to say that the hiring was done too often on my own without prayer. Firing a coach was the worst feeling I have ever experienced. I am glad that those occasions were extremely rare.

Jim Goodman says there is a special bond between coaches. I agree. God blessed me with so many great coaches who remain like family to this day. I have learned much from other coaches, but beyond all the Xs and Os there are five major lessons that stand out. The first was from my head coach at Florida A&M. Rudy Hubbard was a brilliant man with a great work ethic, self-discipline, and compassion for everyone. He taught me to recruit good people. I spent five years under Rudy. Those years began in 1974 with a lot of talent and some good people. We barely ended a five year losing streak by going 6-5. By 1978 we had won two national championships and had the same amount of talent, but the players were very good people. Now Rudy did say, "Get good people who can play, too!"

The next three lessons came from observing Ken Hatfield bring the Lord into the workplace. He encouraged us to be involved in FCA and Bible studies and took some heat at Arkansas for quoting a Bible verse on his TV show. Ken stressed going by all the rules whether good or bad ones because things were done a Christian way or not, and we honored God by our actions in all things. He always said, "The ends don't justify the means."

Ken was a patient leader who taught our young staff how to coach in the midst of adversity. He was positive with us and the team in every meeting through many losses in those first three years at Air Force. He also ingrained in us the wisdom of saying a team must do things better than its opponents or differently. He proved this at the AFA, Arkansas, and Rice with the flexbone offense. This lesson helped us turn LR into a winner after 18 consecutive years of losing.

Hatfield also taught us to continually seek out new knowledge. The atmosphere at the AFA was like a think tank with all the young coaches learning together. We went to the Broncos' practices to learn new schemes, and when we were at Arkansas, some of the coaches he retained from Holtz's former staff had wonderful experience. Jesse Branch taught me how to stop the veer offense. This practice of sharpening our skills was one I continued throughout my coaching career, and I would encourage younger coaches to visit other colleges or bring in experts and to be willing to share what they know with others.

I was also blessed to work for three head coaches: Rudy Hubbard, Ken Hatfield, and Doug Dickey, who believed in coaches having good family lives. Their successful records and championships are proof family life need not be sacrificed in order to win. Coach Dickey established a tradition at Florida on Sundays after church and holidays. All our families were invited to eat at the training table with our players. This brought a true family atmosphere to the staff and team. Ken continued the tradition at his schools, and I was able to continue it at Rice and Duke.

Finally I witnessed an extraordinary decision by Chan Gailey in the winter of 1980. Chan had played quarterback for Coach Dickey at the University of Florida while Ken and I were young coaches on the Florida staff. Chan went on to become a GA at Florida and coach the secondary at Troy State. The day Hatfield got the AFA head job, he hired Chan and me. We roomed together that spring while we were waiting for our families to move up from the South. It was obvious from the start that Chan was a fine coach and the same caring unselfish person he had been as the Gator quarterback and deep snapper. Chan was born in Clarksville, Georgia and was raised in Americus, GA as was his wife Laurie.

By the winter of 1980, we were neighbors on base at the Academy as were all our coaches. We had completed our first season 2- 9, and we were a long way from winning. The end of recruiting was near, and it was the week of the Super Bowl. Chan received a call offering him the secondary job at the University of Florida. They were a great team and the Gaileys would have been close to their parents and definitely would have had a substantial pay increase. Without a doubt, this would have been a no brainer decision for a 28 year old coach with a family. None of us wanted Chan and Laurie to leave, but we didn't anticipate anything else as we awaited his return from Gainesville on Super Bowl Sunday.

That afternoon, Chan came over to the house to watch the game for awhile and was very quiet. I was anxious to hear about the trip. Finally, I burst out asking, "Well what are you going to do?" He calmly informed me, "Oh, I'm staying with Ken." As the defensive coordinator and his close friend, I was ecstatic! However, I had to ask why, and he explained that he was greatly tempted but God had made it plain that the University of Florida atmosphere was not the same as working for Ken Hatfield. Most people would have thought Chan had blown his chance to move forward in his career. Chan honored what God had made clear to him, and God also guided an unwavering Chan Gailey's career just fine. This was a lesson in faith lived out that made an impression on me, and one I hope other young coaches will appreciate. I learned early on that coaches will be happier at schools with good bosses and a family atmosphere. By the way, soon after Chan's decision, the Florida program went on NCAA probation and that coach and his staff were fired. Gailey, of course, went on to be a major part of the AFA's success, a national championship at Troy State, two Super Bowl teams with the Broncos and the Steelers, as well as head coach of the Dallas Cowboys and Georgia Tech, and the current head coach of the Buffalo Bills. These have been Chan's jobs, but in the words of his son Tate, "This is not who he is." Chan is still the same humble man of God, as is Ken Hatfield. They are still examples to another generation of coaches.

What would I have done the same or differently? In retrospect, that's easy. I would have loved to have had more spiritual maturity leading to a closer walk with God in all aspects of life. I would work just as hard to prepare for the games and recruiting as in years past. According to Rudy Hubbard, Woody Hayes said, 'The will to prepare to win is more important than the will to win.' It is the nature of the game for preparation to consume coaches, but I would pray hard to be able to focus on my family's needs and make the short times together during the season quality time. One of my Rice players, Shane Hollas, recently told me that he decided not to get into coaching because he saw all the sacrifices we made and the time it took away from our families. He thought it might be too high a price to pay for a family man. I think it can be done well, but coaches have to make a conscious effort to put their families first.

I would have stayed in the moment and enjoyed each school more without looking ahead. Bob Trott said, "We don't enjoy it when we are there. You are just trying to win. You don't realize until after you leave that you did something special." At FAMU and Florida, I was just happy to be a coach there and to succeed.

At Arkansas the pressure started to hit, and we realized we were in a rat race. I never stopped to smell the roses. Most of us on Hatfield's staff had been together through the AFA and Arkansas and we were like a family. I wish I had been more spiritually mature and enjoyed those relationships at the time instead of letting the pressure overwhelm me.

Most of what I would do the same I learned from Ken as well. He taught me to value the contribution of my assistant coaches. We could disagree in meetings without getting shot down. We knew we always had each other's backs and we should never blame a coach or a player publicly. As a head coach, I tried to listen to the opinions of my coaches and do what was best for the players. Ken treated us like family and let us know what we were doing was important. When players made mistakes, they knew we were for them. It was important to show trust after failure. At Duke, when Scottie Montgomery fumbled in the Northwestern game, we put him back in to show we still had confidence in him. He went on to have a career in the NFL. When B.J. Hill wanted to go into a demanding engineering major, we didn't discourage him even though it meant it would be harder to make the grades and stay eligible. We tried to give each player the same attention after he signed as when he had been a recruit.

I also learned that a coach should never be too busy for people. If someone calls, I will get back to them within 24 hours. I believe no matter how important you think you are, you should never be too busy for people. Once, a parent I had never heard of sent some game film. I watched it and wrote a note back. We didn't have a place for his son, but several weeks later I received an invitation to play at Augusta. It turned out the father was a big executive and wanted to thank me for taking the time to watch the film.

What I tried to stress the most with all the players was character, and I still have the opportunity to do that as a speaker for FCA. Back when we were at Rice, Dallas Cowboys chaplain Tony Evans shared how he always told his children to remember their last name was Evans before they went out. That meant they were representing the family. I started telling my players, "Your last name is Rice." I think it is a good idea to let players know that they represent the team all the time…not just on Saturdays. I reminded David Daly of that principle when he yelled at an official for a bad call. Not only was he representing LR as our chaplain on the sidelines, but he was also wearing an FCA shirt.

FCA allows me to stay involved in football and continue influencing the lives of young men and coaches. It started back in the early 80s at the American Football Coaches convention. Coaches who didn't want to go out partying would meet in a hotel room and share FCA ideas and talk about how to honor God in coaching. Those meetings have now evolved into Sunday morning worship services with approximately 400 coaches. When I was in Florida, the convention and FCA had a coaches' breakfast sponsored by Mack Trucks Inc. Some of the first speakers were J.C. Watts, Tom Osborne and Grant Teaff. It has been a tremendous experience for me to interact with Christian coaches from other staffs.

Not only did we have the convention meetings, but Ken started inviting speakers to talk to our teams. Maryland player Ken Watson, a former teammate of John Zernhelt, spoke at the AFA. Watson also spoke to my teams at Duke, Rice, and LR.

R.V. Brown, the Gators chaplain, had made an incredible impact at Appalachian and NC State, so I invited him to talk to our Lenoir Rhyne team. Many of our players accepted Christ that day. Carey Casey spoke to our Arkansas, Rice, and Duke teams. It was special to have him do a joint share time with both our team and Carson Newman during the 2009 season at Lenoir Rhyne.

My relationships with godly coaches and players have helped me keep my eyes on God, and if you keep your eyes on God you can stay on an even keel despite the good and bad times- the peaks when everyone loves you and the valleys when they all hate you. I learned not to take the criticism or the praise too seriously. I was no more of a miracle worker at Rice than I was the Sports Illustrated Bonehead Coach of the Week. I would tell coaches never to start believing your own press and take your eyes off God.

This book is about the life of a football coach, but it is also about the relationship I have with Jesus Christ. If you are not sure if you have a relationship with Jesus Christ or you do not know if you would spend eternity in Heaven if you were to die today, you can know for sure by praying a simple prayer like this one:

> God, I am a sinner. I'm sorry for my sin. Forgive me. I want to turn from my sin. I receive Jesus Christ as my Savior; I confess Him as my Lord. From now on I want to follow Him. In Jesus' Name, Amen.

If you prayed that prayer and want to know what to do next, contact your local church. I would also encourage coaches and athletes who want to learn more about what it means to be a Christian to get involved in FCA chapters in their local schools. The motto of FCA is Faith, Family, Football, and those priorities will help any coach succeed in the game of life.

The End Zone

At the end of our driveway is a sign that says "Fred and Pam's End Zone". It is hard to believe all those years of moving and football are behind us. We finally have a permanent home in Franklin. In this final chapter, the children and I would like to add our thoughts to Fred's because football has been a way of life for our entire family.

I'd like to say just a word about my take on our newlywed days. Ah, marriage is wonderful, but ... it is by the grace of God that we married or ever stayed married. We were too young to be married, but we did love each other. We had somewhat different views on everything and had many disagreements. The week before the wedding, I was still praying and considering whether or not to marry Fred. I walked the aisle in church but was young in the Christian faith, and I knew I could not marry someone who did not know the Lord. It was important that my husband shared my faith, especially since we were opposites in almost every other way. We had a lovely big wedding. Then I went back to the excitement of learning how to be a coach's wife.

It was an adventure for both of us. I always considered his job must come first. I never complained about the long days and late hours spent pouring over film. I maintained it was just what was expected to be a good coach and make a good living. I always loved being a mom and taking care of our girls. When Fred began getting job offers to other schools it was just accepted fact that we would need to pack up, sell the house and move again. I think at last count it was 27 houses. When I look back at those days, I think how foolish it seemed at times to move, and I wonder whether it was right or wrong to pay the price to advance. But we were happy and not always consulting the Lord about His plans for us. Even under those circumstances God was watching over us.

The coaching staffs with whom we associated were wonderful blessings. The Air Force Academy was the furthest away from our families. The coaches and their wives became like family as we met during the games and rooted on our team. A real camaraderie developed as the games weren't just fun afternoons. They were personal and about the players, problems, and our livelihoods. When you know that if you don't win enough games you will probably be fired, it affects one's mindset. We all lived together on base in cul-de-sac housing. I still have so many dear friends from those days.

As I reflect on that time, I am so proud of my husband. By His grace, God shaped Fred into a man after God's heart. He is truly a caring person and a stickler for returning phone calls. So many times the phone rings late at night with a younger coach on the other end of the line asking for help with a job or help with a difficult situation. Working with The Fellowship of Christian Athletes has brought great joy to his life and mine as we watch coaches and players come into a relationship with Jesus Christ.

In Colorado, God blessed me in another unexpected way. Through a prayer uttered as I was driving down that beautiful mountain range by the Academy, I asked the Lord if He could use me in something to do for Him. Through an unbelievable set of circumstances, he impressed upon me to start a ministry called Community Care Center. We helped people with immediate needs, it grew with many stories of God's goodness, and the Gospel was always shared with those who would listen.

From there as we moved to other universities, I would get that prompting and start another ministry for families. Each one would grow, and with prayer, workers would show up to help. We really didn't have to ask for anything. We would just pray and all the needs would be met. What a privilege it is to know God does care for each one of us, and He is very personal.

As our life has made a big circle, I would certainly say Fred and I have had our ups and downs. In those younger years, we did not see eye to eye on much. I have my way of doing things, Fred has his, and they seldom seem to mesh. I remember right after the wedding we were returning to our newly rented garage apartment at the University of Florida. We were in our red VW Bug, and I had to have the windows up in the sweltering heat with no AC because I didn't want to mess up my hair. That was our first argument that day. As we began unloading the car I started looking for my shoes. They were in garbage bags we were using as luggage. Fred gave away my shoes! My shoes! I couldn't believe it! By God's grace we have made it this far.

Now we are blessed with two wonderful daughters and fantastic sons-in-law. Our four grandchildren keep us busy and laughing. I guess as one gets older, the things that seemed so important in earlier years just fade away a bit, and, hopefully, we find that place in the middle of God's will. We do laugh about the shoes now. I must say we agree on most things. My Coach is the love of my life. We are blessed, always have been, but now really know the great goodness of God. To Him be the glory forever. Psalm 126:3 "The Lord has done great things for us and we are filled with joy."

Pamela Goldsmith

For many, Saturday is a break from a long work week. For the daughter of a football coach it is much more stressful. As fans filled the stadium laughing with friends, our family sat together, a bundle of nerves, quietly praying over the safety of our players. I've often compared our life to the moment when the kicker kicks a field goal. The ball seems to hang in the air while all spectators hold their breath awaiting the outcome. Week after week we hope and pray for a win because it's not just a game; Dad's job depends on it. I can remember watching a Razorback game when Dad was the defensive coordinator and hearing the crowd chant, "Fred, Fred, Fred, Fred" because the defense couldn't be beat that day. I looked to my mother and said, "Isn't it great?" She looked at me unable to enjoy the moment because she knew the crowds could turn on a dime. Boy was she right. Just a few weeks later we heard, "Fire Fred! Fire Fred!" It made me mad and I turned around and let the elderly couple who started the chant know that I didn't appreciate them speaking about my father that way. Thankfully, they kept quiet the rest of the game.

The benefits far outweighed the negatives. For example, we went to bowl games every Christmas break for almost my entire childhood. Our family was able to stay in lovely hotels, take excursions to Sea World and Disney World, and see all the local sights. The food was delicious. We had gift baskets with chocolate and candy in our hotel rooms. At the Cotton Bowl, the whole bed was decorated with gift baskets every day. I also enjoyed the hotel arcade rooms. I'd challenge players on my favorite games and then play them over and over while they had to attend football practice. They would come back and find their high scores beaten. My birthday is two days after Christmas, so my dad always had the hotel bring me a piece of cake with a candle to celebrate. My friends enjoyed the benefits as well. They loved coming to games on the bus with me because we had police escorts. We whizzed through red lights as people stood along the streets cheering for our team. It was a great life full of interesting people and places.

However, it wasn't always easy. The hardest part of being a coach's kid can be the transient lifestyle. I attended three different elementary schools and two high schools. Though difficult, those experiences did make it easier for me to handle interacting with different groups of people. Mom and Dad did everything in their power to make the transitions smooth for us. We always treated the moves like family adventures. My mom handled most of the moving so Dad could get started in his new position. The hours coaches work are insane, so their wives shoulder a lot of responsibility. The wives and kids spend every Saturday together either attending home games or listening to away games on the radio. The entire staff becomes one big family.

Being a football coach doesn't leave much time for family since everything in life is planned around football season and recruiting. But, somehow my Dad found time to help me practice hitting and fielding for my little league baseball team. I received pointers on how to hang in there with the boys since I was the only girl on the team. He always encouraged me in whatever I wanted to do. Even though he wasn't home much, he wanted to be involved in my life. He protected me from boys who wouldn't have been good for me, put up with my crushes on his players, and embarrassingly enough, even set me up with my amazing husband.

Dad also prayed with me regularly, and he prays diligently for others as well. He has a file folder with names written under every day of the week. If your name is on there, then he will pray for you literally until you go to be with the Lord. Dad has such an amazing heart and love for people. He quickly forgives and doesn't hold a grudge. He challenged me to learn scripture and quizzed me on it. The one I remember him wanting me to learn the most was Philippians 4:6-7 because we were both worriers. There is not a single conversation that I have had with him that doesn't end in his famous words, "It'll all work out."

Even though Dad is a great guy, nothing impresses me more than his desire to see people come to know the Lord. Over the years, students, players, and coaches have been missing something in their life. When they shared their hearts with Dad, he listened and let them know there was hope, not hope in school or football, but hope in something much greater - Jesus Christ. Numerous men and women will live eternally with God because Fred Goldsmith was faithful. He was a faithful son to a single mother in a wheelchair, and he is a faithful husband to his high school sweetheart, a faithful father to his daughters, and a faithful servant of the Almighty God. Robin Goldsmith Park

Although it was difficult to have Dad gone so much and move 13 times as a child, I wouldn't trade being a coach's daughter. I loved all excitement that went along with the job, and always knew I could find Dad at his office. During my freshman year of college at Arkansas, my dorm was right across the street from our athletic complex, and I used stop by and see Dad on my way to class.

The players were like big brothers to me. I appreciated that most of the time. Once, my old red Mustang got stuck in a ditch and some of the guys got it out for me. Sometimes they could be overprotective. For example, my husband had a class with Ted Shimer. When Joel told Ted he was going to ask me out, the linebacker said, "You can't do that. He'll kill you!" My favorite memories are of eating with the team at the training table and waiting by the locker room after the games.

The downside was that we had to plan everything around football, even getting engaged and married. When Joel wanted to ask for my hand, Dad was so busy getting ready for the Cotton Bowl in 1988 that he had him come to his office at 6:00a.m.to talk to him. He was preoccupied and didn't realize why my boyfriend would want to talk to him (coaches go into a fog before big games and it's the best time to ask for anything). Coach Trott figured it out and was listening in since his office was next door. Dad thought Joel was there to ask for Cotton Bowl tickets. I wanted to get married over winter break, but that would have interfered with recruiting, so we had to pick the only date in July that Dad could make it.

During those years at the AFA and the U of A, we truly were as close to our staff as our own extended family, and spent more time with them. My parents only had one sibling each. They lived far away, so the coaches and their wives were like my aunts and uncles.

I used to babysit for the Gaileys when I was in middle school. I really looked up to Laurie. She didn't have daughters, and we lived across the street, so she made my sister and me Christmas ornaments. She and Coach Gailey had been high school sweethearts and she used to read me their old love letters. I remember Coach Gailey being there to see my reaction when my parents had my dog flown in from Florida. I also babysat for the Trotts when Amanda was an adorable toddler. When her dad was with my dad at Duke, she babysat for my girls.

Sandy Hatfield helped me pick out my first horse. Since all the other kids on our staff were little kids until Michelle DeBerry came, and I was at that awkward preteen age, Sandy let me sit in her box at the games. I loved going to the Hatfields because they had an old fashioned Coke machine in their basement. When I was a newlywed, my mother had moved away to Texas and Sandy had me over and taught me how to cook some of her best recipes.

This book originally started out as a project to record Dad's memories for the family. For years, I have wanted to record Dad's stories. As we began writing, he kept telling me I needed to talk to other people that were there, and we realized it is not only his story; it is the story of all the people he worked with. As a result, many names are included. Some of them, our readers may have never heard of, but the goal was never to limit his stories to ones about famous people in order to sell books. It was important to Dad to include everyone who has meant something to him throughout his career. We chose to publish this book to give Dad a chance to thank all the men who have shaped and molded his life. I hope it will help shape and mold the lives of others as well.

It has been a privilege to reconnect with many of the players and coaches from our past and hear their perspectives. I am proud of my Dad and am thankful that this book has given him an opportunity few ever experience. He now knows the impact his life has had on others.

Kimberly Goldsmith McDaniel

Acknowledgments

I was blessed to have been coached by and coached with some great men. I would like to close by naming all of them because without their many ways of helping, the journey would never have worked. I would also like to thank Les Todd and Duke Photography for providing the cover photo and Mike Burrows for offering editorial advice. Finally, I want to thank my daughter Kim for conducting all the interviews and writing my story.

My childhood coaches and the Miami Southwest Boy's Club: Bob Graham, Joe Atwood, and Don Griffiths. My high school JV coaches were: Gary Ghormley, Dave Wood, Bob McCabe, and Dan Finoa. The Coral Gables varsity staff was the best I've ever seen. They were: Nick Kotys, Joe Krutulis, Ed Injaychock, Jack McCloskey, Sam Scarnechia, and Ed Stockel. My college coaches at Western Carolina were: Dan Robinson, Tom Young, Bob Setzer and Jimmy Lovett. I worked with the aforementioned Gables staff in my first coaching job and Danny Coughlin was also one of our coaches at that time. Next, our great staff at Gainesville High School included: Jim Niblack,

Wesley Dicks, Hurley Manning, Jack Jones, Robert Davis, Fritchie Smith, Loren Giannamore, and Garney Hatch. My first staff as a head coach at Hamilton County, Florida included: George Sapp, Harold Bethea, Dave Lawrence, and Dr. Fred Mickler. As an assistant at Coral Park in Miami, I coached with: Frank Downing, Bob Irvin, Fred Cooley, Gary Rapp, Don Soldinger, Bob Martin, and Dave Lawrence. When I got my big break as a head coach at Charlotte County High School, I worked with Mike Lay, David Lawrence, Gary Rapp, Jack Card, Mike Eader, Bill Seidel, Joey Kennedy, Chuck Field, and Dick Santello.

As a GA at the University of Florida, I worked with: Doug Dickey, Jimmy Dunn, Doug Knotts, Jack Thompson, Ken Hatfield, Jimmy Haines, Don Deal, Jack Hall, Lindy Infante, Don Brown, Bill Carr, Alan Trammell, Charley Fulton, Jim Blackburn, and Chris Patrick.

At Deland High School our staff included: Bill Carr, Dave Hiss, Rocky Cottrell, Jim Wise, Gil Dominquez, Bruce Greathouse, George Dominquez, Tony Tussing, Frank Harwood, Les Valerie, and our great athletic director, Spec Martin.

My big break as a college assistant gave me a chance to coach with: Rudy Hubbard, Alan Bogan, Costa Kittles, Bobby Lang, Mark Orlando, Bob Mungen, Amos Hill, Pete Griffin, Ice Man Henderson, Earl Goodman, trainer George Thompson, athletic director Hansel Tookes, football secretary Lillian

Hagins, and Sports Information Director Roosevelt
Wilson.

Next came the AFA with: Ken Hatfield, Fisher
DeBerry, Chan Gailey, Bob Trott, AL Groh, Dick
Bumpass, Wally Ake, Tom Backhus, Don
Blackwelder, Roger Hinshaw, Larry Brinson, Ed Hutt,
Dick Ellis, Jim Bowman, Jim Goodman, Sammy
Steinmark, Dick Enga, Larry Beckman, Billy Mitchell,
Carl Russ, great athletic director John Clune, legendary
trainers Jim Conboy, and Joe Smith and our equipment
man, Levi Pee Wee Cordova.

Our Arkansas staff was: Ken Hatfield, Bob Trott,
Wally Ake, Roger Hinshaw, Larry Brinson, Larry
Beckman, David Lee, Jesse Branch, Ken Turner, John
Stuckey George Williford, Gene Smith, Ed Orgeron,
Houston Nutt, Keith Burns, Chuck Peterson, Danny
Nutt, Mark Cordelli, Mike Vaught, Larry Dixon, Ron
Schroeder, John Bond, Mike Falleur, Randy Owens,
Scott Reed, athletic director Frank Broyles, Assistant
AD Terry Don Phillips, the chaplain of the
Razorbacks, H.D. McCarty, and trainer Dean Weber.

Slippery Rock: George Mihalik, Doug Clinger, Stan
Kendziorski, Paul Bruno, Jeff McInerney, Bruce
Boliver, Rod Oberlin, Vic Campagna, and trainer Cory
Odom, and AD Bob Oliver.

Rice: Craig Bohl, Mike Heimerdinger, Scott Conley,
Dean Campbell, Mike Bender, John Zernhelt, Keith
Burns, Dave Cope, Joe DeForest, Will Taylor, Ryan
Strong, Steve Kidd, Joe Heikinen, Bob Barrett, Tim
Fitzpatrick, Kirk Thor, Les Koenning, Everett

Coleman, David Moody, Ted Gill, Hardee McCrary,
Steve Carson. Trainers- Jimmy Roton and Allen
Eggert. Athletic director Bobby May, equipment
manager Jackie Miles, Strength coaches Jeff Madden
andKeith Irwin, Beth Stringham, Sports Information
Director, Bill Cousins, Academic advisors David Moss
and Julie Griswold, and Matt Musil media.

Duke: Craig Bohl, Mike Heimerdinger, Jeff
McLInerney Larry Beckish, John Zernheldt, Ken
Matous, Les Koenning, Rod Broadway, Jimmy
Gonzales, Doug Knotts, John Xhizmar, Sonny
Falcone, Greg Willig, Joe DeForrest, Clint Park, Nick
Miller, Carlisle Mabery, John MacDonald, Shirley
Rigsbee, Mickey Laws, Mary Dinkins, Fred Chatham,
Greg Williams, Brad Sherrod, Joe DeLaumielleure, Joe
D'Alessandris, Scott Brown, Bob Trott, athletic
director Tom Butters, assistant A.D. Joe Alleva, Sports
Information Director Mike Cragg, Chris Kennedy and
Brad Berndt in academic, equipment manager Mike
Hawley, trainer Hap Zarzour, Bob Harris, media.

Franklin High School: Josh Brooks, Jay Brooks, Bob
Kuppers, Tony Plemmons, Kris Reis, Bill Crane, Kyle
Garner, Blake Harrell, Todd Gibbs, Todd Leek, Gene
Young, Mickey Carpenter, Gary Brown, Kevin Sinden,
Mike Wood, Eddie Trull, Warren Winchester, Ben
Van Hook, Mark Young, Dale Hough, Charley Keely,
Reddy Hughes, Ryan Raby, Mark Sutton, Eddie Trull

Lenoir Rhyne: Mike Houston, Brian Hill, Blake
Harrell, Kyle Garner, Roy Tesh, Brent Thompson,
Alan Gerber, Brain Rucker, Chris Coleman, Rod

Stephens, Ron Boyd, Trent Lowman, Chuck Robinson, Aaron Brock, Tarron Williams, Brad McLaughterty, Lou Conte, Athletic Director Neill McGeachy, Trainer Mike McGee, chaplains David Daly, Lance Shealy and Dale Watts.

Thanks God
for the memories

With my brother David at
Coral Gables Elementary

Pam & I at the prom

1961 Coral Gables HS, 11 players played Div I College football

Our family in Houston before grandkids

Our family in
Franklin after
grandkids

With Kim's
twins, Kinsey
& Kayla
McDaniel

Robin's
children,
Abby Paige &
Gavin Park

Joe Atwood our coach, inspired me to be a coach

Chan and Laurie Gailey on 1980 AFA Hawaii trip

Air Force Academy staff with Thunderbirds 1983

1989 with Tom Landry, legend and role model, at a Houston FCA luncheon

Harold Mack (FSU), Dallas Cowboy VP Gil Brandt, Burton Lawless (Gators and Cowboys). They were all influential in our futures.

Billy Granville (Duke) vs FSU, NFL LB
with Bengals and Texans

2007 Hall of Fame Profile

Fred Goldsmith

Coach • 1974-79

Under the leadership of Coach Fred Goldsmith, the Florida A&M Defense became one of the nation's most formidable units in the late 1970s, providing much of the spark behind the Rattlers' 44-11-2 record during his five-year tenure.

FAMU finished as the nation's only unbeaten team in 1977, posting an 11-0 standard, capturing the Black College National title, before winning the inaugural NCAA Division I-AA national crown in 1978, led by the nation's number one defense.

•In 46 games over four season from 1975 to 1978, Goldsmith's defensive units held opposing teams to one score or less 20 times, including eight (8) shutouts.

•In 1975, the Rattler Defense ranked #2 in NCAA Division Two in scoring defense, allowing just 6.3 points per game, with four (4) shutouts, sparking FAMU to a 9-2 finish.

•In 1978, FAMU led NCAA Division I-AA in both total defense, allowing 149.9 yards per game and rushing defense, surrendering just 48.6 yards per contest, with four (4) shutouts.

Goldsmith helped develop three All-America defenders during his stint at Florida A&M; linebacker Frankie Poole (1975); defensive end Jeff Grady (1977) and noseguard Harrell Oliver (1978), while nearly a dozen Rattlers earned All-Southern Intercollegiate Athletic Conference honors during his time.

FAMU Hall of Fame

Pam looking on as Rice All American Trevor Cobb
receives the Doak Walker award.

FOOTBALL COACHES — Left to Right: Gary Rapp, Mike Eader, Mike Lay, Fred Goldsmith (Head), Jack Card, Chuck Field and Bill Seidel.

FIRST ROW: Harold Mack, Reggie Carr, Randi Keiser, Burton Lawless, Robert Horton, Ed Stepp, Van Henry. SECOND ROW: Stafford Bryant, Mike Haymans, Kenny Poteet, Marlon Runkle, Pete Whisenant, John Herlovich, Bruce Dooley. THIRD ROW: Charles Bryant, Booker T. Haynes, Sandy Burke, Ben Graham, Wayne Sallade, Wendell Woolum, Paul DeGaeta, Harold Weaver. FOURTH ROW: Spike Anderson, Bill Sindledecker, Norm Anderson, Jim McCurry, Jeff Gilmore, Rick Lewis, and Dale Russell. Also, Randy Sisk.

1970 Tarpons Team

Pam and I at Texas Stadium during CFA meetings

Ken and I working on AFCA coaches retirement in DC with
Arkansas Senator David Pryor

With Jackie Robinson
in 1954

1995 Razorback
staff

BOBBY DODD
COACH OF THE YEAR
AWARD

Presented to

FRED GOLDSMITH

March 1, 1995

In recognition of a high and more noble aspect of college coaching . . . a style that emphasizes something more than winning the game. . . a belief that the game of football should be kept in perspective with college life in general.

It was a great honor to be associated with Bobby Dodd

At Augusta with Razorback John Daly in the mid 90's

With Duke QB
Spence Fisher

FAMU two
time National
Championship
Coach Rudy
Hubbard

First Head job in Jasper, FL 1967

Steve Spurrier and Jack Card visiting our Jasper team

FAMU linebackers, defensive ends 1974

Rick Porter (Squeaky) All American
1981, Lions and Colts NFL

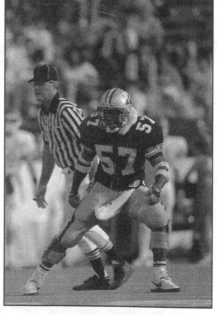

OJ Brigance, a great leader and
"difference maker" in changing
Rice's football culture. NFL and
CFL all star courageously battling
Lou Gehrig's disease.

1994 Duke Bowl team and staff

Dal Shealy, Tony Dungy at NFL Combine 2012

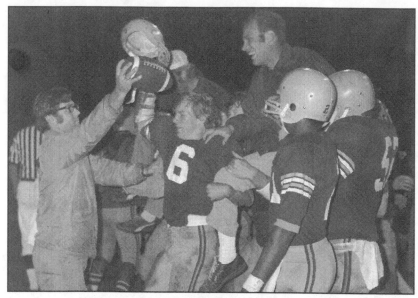

DeLand Bulldogs going to 1972 Christmas Bowl, Coach Tony Tussing
with game ball, #6 Frank Calkins, Willie Clark.

First game at Lenoir Rhyne, 2007

With Boo Boo Weaver in 1969

Ken tries to dump me off a jet ski at Chan's lake house. You can tell we are happily retired!

Retired and enjoying winning the FCA Tournament in Franklin with
Vic Teague, Pete Penland, Chris Hedden & Steve Penland

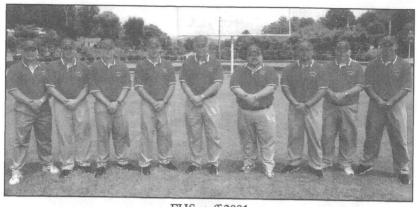

FHS staff 2001

LR staff - Mike Houston, Brent Thompson, Blake Harrell, Ron Boyd, Chris Collins, Kyle Garner, Taron Williams, Aaron Brock, Roy Tesh

These "Brothers" made a difference sharing Jesus with the LR staff and players!

Lance Shealy
FCA Director

David Daly
Team Chaplain

Dale Watts
Team Chaplain

1992 Rice staff - Craig Bohl, Mike Heimerdinger, John Zernhelt, Les Koenning, David Moody, Joe DeForest, Keith Burns, Bryant Poole, Jeff McInerney

Made in the USA
Charleston, SC
26 October 2012